D1107582

A

DWARFED

TREE

MANUAL

FOR

WESTERNERS

# A DWARFED TREE

# MANUAL

*for*

# WESTERNERS

*by*

## Samuel Newsom

TOKYO NEWS SERVICE, LTD.
Tokyo, Japan

Copyright: All rights reserved

© Samuel Newsom

*Published Nov. 1960*
*Second Printing June 1962*
*Third Printing September 1962*
*Revised Edition—September 1963*


U.S.A. Library of Congress Catalog Card Number: 60-16497

*Printed in Japan*
TOKYO NEWS SERVICE, LTD.

Kosoku-doro, Bldg., Ginza-nishi,
Chuo-ku, Tokyo, Japan
*Layout and Typography by D. E. Woelfer*

# INTRODUCTION

About sixty miles from Tokyo, close to the town of Omiya, is a remarkable place known throughout Japan as "Bonsai Machi" or "Dwarfed Tree Village." Here are located several dwarfed tree farms devoted exclusively to the production of these miniature living gems, and here one can see some of the best dwarfed trees in Japan. To those interested in this hobby, a trip to "Bonsai Machi" would be worth all the expense and time required even though it took years of planning. There is something about seeing things at the source, and with one's own eyes that cannot be equalled. However, as such a trip is entirely out of the question for practically all of us, no matter how enthused we may be, we are by necessity forced to rely upon available local material for our information.

About ten years ago, at the beautifully wooded town of Mill Valley in California, the author started what he calls his "Bonsai En" or "Dwarfed Tree Garden." It began in a modest way as a place for a small collection of dwarfed trees, but as the years passed it became crowded with little trees in all stages of development, so a section of "The Greenwood Tree," the author's shop in Mill Valley has also turned into a display garden for these. Although the present collection was started only ten years ago, it includes quite a number of older specimens and is the direct result of over thirty years of growing bonsai.

It is a great satisfaction to be able to include a full description of the "Bonsai En" in this book, as it shows, as no Western book on dwarfing has done, a practical Western set-up for the production of dwarfed trees in relatively large numbers. At present about fifteen hundred trees of all ages and sizes are being cared for at the "Bonsai En."

So, in a measure this book is a fairly good substitute for a trip to the Japanese "Bonsai Machi." It has this added advantage—it's all in English. The inclusion of such things as rocks and driftwood collecting is an added Western touch which should lead on to the development of an entirely new form of dwarfed tree arranging. The author wishes you the greatest pleasure with this book, whether read for the sake of relaxation, or as a guide in your dwarfing activities.

Good luck!

SAM'L NEWSOM

MILL VALLEY, CALIFORNIA

## Acknowledgements

Special thanks are due the following who greatly helped in the bringing together of much new and unusual material for this book.

Dr. Jiro Harada of the National Museum in Tokyo, for his beautiful photographs of the older Bonsai, taken by himself, many in the famous "Bonsai Machi" or "Dwarfed Tree Village" near Omiya, Japan.

Mr. Lew Tyrrel, for the photos of the author's dwarfed tree garden, and for a great number of other illustrations. His personal interest and enthusiasm added much to the special character of this volume.

The San Francisco Examiner in allowing the use of several excellent shots of the "Repotting and Trimming" of nursery stock (Chapter 2), and the illustration showing the growth of a Bonsai from a cutting to a mature specimen.

Also most helpful were several books on Bonsai written in Japanese. These have been a fruitful source of information as to Japanese methods, and the Japanese philosophical background. (see bibliography)

# CONTENTS

## CHAPTER 1

## ELEMENTS OF DWARFED TREE CULTURE

## CHAPTER 2

## COLLECTION, PROPAGATION, AND TRAINING

## CHAPTER 3

## CONSTRUCTION OF THE DWARFED TREE GARDEN

# CHAPTER 4

## NEEDLE-BEARING TREES

# CHAPTER 5

## BROAD LEAVED AND DECIDUOUS TREES

# LIST OF ILLUSTRATIONS

*Chinese Juniper about fifteen years old, displayed on a Redwood plank table.*

# CHAPTER 1.

## *Elements of Dwarfed Tree Culture*

### 1.   THE WESTERNER AND DWARFED TREES

From the average Westerner's viewpoint, no presentation of things Japanese is complete without a description of Bonsai or dwarfed trees; but while many Americans are interested in these miniature giants of the forest, they seem to think their culture is beyond the comprehension of all but Japanese gardeners. The usual viewpoint is "Of course dwarfed trees do well in Japan, but Westerners would have no luck with them." For many years the writer has been enthusiastically investigating the cult and culture of the dwarfed tree, and hopes this book will prove that Westerners can raise their own and become followers of an exceedingly interesting hobby.

To one who has a general knowledge of gardening, the dwarfing of various shrubs and trees, and the transforming of uninteresting plants into objects of beauty, should not be difficult. Dwarfed trees are, after all but pot plants, and there is hardly a person interested in gardening who hasn't had a degree of success with potted flowers or plants. Certain general rules apply to all vegetation. Pots must not be allowed to dry, plants must be periodically fertilized and trimmed, and so on, but the growing of dwarfed trees, as trees, seems to be a new idea to most, so, first of all, let us examine the Oriental background, and the Oriental thinking that gives vitality to this satisfying hobby.

Why do the Japanese like dwarfed trees? To obtain a satisfactory answer to this question, we must strike directly at the taproot of Japanese culture and philosophy. The Japanese way of life, in contrast to the Western idea of hewing down forests and creating cities and abodes of men, is to flow along with nature, in perfect subordination to fundamental natural laws. The fable of the Oak and the Reed could be a representation of Eastern and Western cultures; The Westerner, like the Oak, faces the storm, though his limbs be torn and broken; but the more pliant Oriental bows to the flood and the gales of heaven, and, reed-like, escapes destruction.

This love of nature—this awareness of a oneness with living things, permeates and colors all the classical culture of Japan. From it have sprung the noble art of gardening and such popular studies as flower arranging, tray landscapes and love of miniature stones. The fine arts strongly reflect the influence of natural forms, as do all other branches of Japanese endeavor. For instance there is no type of architecture more natural in conception than the Japanese. How logical it is that even trees are modified to fit into this cultural pattern; dwarfed to represent far forests or trained on stones to simulate the sea with its islands, or rocky peaks and other exotic scenes. All for the maintenance of the ever important contact with nature for those compelled to live in crowded cities far from such soul-satisfying surroundings.

There is a quaintness, an antique charm about dwarfed trees. When properly displayed their ancient trunks, contrasting foliages and artistic containers form harmonious rhythms that are exceedingly pleasing. No wonder thousands of Orientals devote their spare time to this hobby: training, dwarfing and displaying beautiful miniature trees. Each year sees an increasing number of the devotees of this art. When exhibitions are held in such cities as Tokyo whole buildings are given over to the great numbers of trees brought together to compete for prizes in various classes. Crowds of people go to admire and to study; pictures are taken of the winning trees; books are published and such occasions are major cultural events.

Dwarfed trees are not grown for beauty alone. While loveliness is an important characteristic, they inevitably suggest much more. The following classifications explain some of the points sought for in good trees. The writer collected these from popular Japanese books on the subject. They reflect the general ideas of Japanese dwarfed tree growers.

## 2.  JAPANESE CLASSIFICATIONS OF DWARFED TREES

1.  Evergreens to be admired the entire four seasons of the year.
2.  Trees with flowers whose greatest beauty is in the Spring.
3.  Trees with flowers that bloom in the Summer.
4.  Trees with flowers that open in Autumn.
5.  Trees with flowers to be enjoyed in the Winter.
6.  Trees and plants to be admired for the beauty of their budding foliages and new sprouts in Spring.
7.  Plants grown for their cool, lush green foliages in Summer.
8.  Trees and plants which exhibit colorful Autumn foliages.
9.  Fruit and berry-bearing trees and plants (Summer, Autumn, Winter).
10. Trees with interesting trunks and branches, to be shown in their naked Winter condition.

A second classification has to do with structure. As trunks are considered the most important single feature, trees are divided as follows:

Upright trunks, such as one finds on trees growing by themselves in a meadow.

Slanting trunks, half cascading effects as if the trees were reaching out from a steep slope.

Gnarled and twisted trunks, like those on trees exposed to the gales of some mountain peak.

Weeping or hanging trunks, as found in trees growing downward from crevices in cliffs.

Then there is the classification according to the numbers of trees planted together, as follows:

Two trunks.

Three trunks.

Five trunks.

Trees planted so close together they seem to be springing from the same stump.

Root connected, where the same roots have several trunks springing from them.

Planted on stones, trees with roots trained over stones.

Some trees have but one feature, while others combine two, three, and even four classifications.

## 3. POTS FOR DWARFED TREES

The proper displaying of dwarfed trees calls for absolute harmony of tree and surroundings. There is a special mutual interdependence between a tree and its container; the points of color and form and the character of both the tree and the pot must be studied, and care used in their combining. If these things are neglected, even a magnificent tree will lose much of its charm and value. The container should reflect and support the beauty of the tree planted in it.

*A selection of Japanese pots for dwarfed trees*

It follows that the enthusiast spends considerable time in the selection of proper containers. So to become an expert in the culture of dwarfed trees one learns about porcelains and pottery.

The most highly prized containers are antique Chinese and Korean pots and trays. Large sums are gladly paid for just the right kind. For those interested in the names of the different types of porcelain and pottery used by the Japanese there are the Chinese and Korean, Nankin, Korai, Kinyo, Kanto, Nanban, Shudei, Shidei, Udei, Kaiso, Rihidei and Sangoyo. Among the Japanese containers most eagerly sought are ancient Seto, Old Bizen, Old Satsuma, Shinraku and others less widely known.

These pots are divided into color groups. There are yellow, white, lavender, red, coral, lapis, grey, black and intermediate shades. Official colors are five: white, black, red, blue-green and yellow. However the amateur will not at first be interested in the purchase of such rare and costly objects, but will content himself with the popularly priced containers now on the market and used by the great majority of dwarfed tree growers, or will make his own containers of wood. If one is attempting the construction of finished containers, a mitre box is essential, but unless special precautions are taken, the mitred corners, being wet on the inside and sunbaked on the outside, will tend to pull apart. Experience has shown that the amateur is more successful when designing containers of hand split wood, put together in a rustic manner. A useful point is the making of drainage holes in the corners, and not in the middle of containers, as those in the middle are in the way of roots when repotting. Most containers being quite shallow, this is important.

As to what color combinations are good, here a few examples: for Pines, Junipers and other evergreens, containers having suggestions of green, grey, lavender, brown or dark greens harmonize well. For flowering trees, the flowers determine the color. White Plums sometimes look well in black pots; red Plums in white pots. Budding Maples are shown in containers of a white or cream nature but at the time of red Autumn foliages are planted in green and blue shades. Plants, grasses and such things, when combined with water and ornamental stones, look well in yellow containers, and the blue and emerald shaded pots are exceptionally attractive when spread with white sand, with trees planed on stones placed in them.

Particularly striking and appropriate combinations noted at various exhibitions included a Flowering Quince in a cream container, a Five-Needled Pine planted in a low tray of rough dark brown glaze, a Chinese Juniper in a deep green tray that matched the foliage, long-needled Pine in a rectangular pot of a pale greyed lavender with the corners indented, a pink flowering Peach in a white pot, another Pine in a light brown container, and a Jasmine in a pale round greenish grey pot that blended beautifully with the blossoms. From these examples it can be seen that there are no hard and fixed rules, each exhibitor using his own judgement as to what seems best. In general it is a good idea to use pots of lighter shades for flowering things, and darker pots for evergreens, though even here one finds exceptions.

Looking at the potting of dwarfed trees from the point of shape, those with straight trunks, and those assembled in groups as miniature forests, appear best in long rectangular shallow trays. For emphasizing graceful lines, square and oval pots are best. Round containers of fairly good depth are excellent for trees trained to hang downward, as if growing from cliffs and also for bamboo and other things interesting in Summer, though most grasses are planted in shallow, round pots.

Considering the shapes of the pots themselves there are rectangular, square, six-sided, eight-sided, diamond shaped, counter diamond shaped (with corners cut in), elliptical, round, those with fancy edges of various designs, melon shaped, leaf shaped, cylindrical, and other miscellaneous kinds. The most common are the rectangular, square and round forms.

Keeping the above mentioned varieties of pots and their colors in mind, one can visualize the problems presented to the grower of dwarfed trees who wishes to display specimens of his art. Pots of appropriate colors must not only be selected, but harmonizing trees and pots must be displayed with reference to others grouped about them. This leads on to another phase of dwarfed tree culture, the study of rare woods and the design and selection of wooden stands upon which to show the finished specimens.

## 4.   TABLES AND STANDS

Stands do away with monotony and bring out the beauty and dignity of the trees. There are stands and low tables of all conceivable varieties. Usually the tables seen in exhibitions are rectangular with rather short legs, not over a foot in height. They are a little wider than the ordinary Japanese tables. In the higher stands there are some with four or six sides, others shaped like plum blossoms, others of irregular shapes. Some legs are of carved woods cut in a natural manner. Others are carved in ornamental designs. Finally many flat boards are used for certain plants. Old weatherbeaten boards from boats and water wheels, artistically joined, make excellent flat stands. Bamboo mats, like little log rafts are frequently seen, as are all sorts of unusual and fascinating slices of highly polished woods, sometimes with irregular edges and sometimes squared.

These stands and tables conform to the style of the trees being exhibited upon them. Trees trained to resemble those growing from cliffs are placed on tall stands; the low wide tables are used for trees with straight trunks, for those grouped together like miniature woods and forests and for individual specimens. The flat boards are used for grasses and other plants in shallow containers.

*Some tables and stands combined with completed dwarfed trees.*

A. Azalea on a tall stand made from a root. (Rhododendron indicum)

B. Gumi (Silver Berry) on a tall formal stand. (Kadsura Japonica)

C. A Wax Tree on a low table. (Rhus sylvestris)

D. Ezo Spruces on a very low table. (Picea hondoensis)

## 5.  INCENSE BURNERS

Incense burners are also seen at dwarfed tree exhibitions. They are an important Oriental item, imparting a solemn and quiet taste to the finished grouping, as if the trees were being shown in a private residence. Incense burners are generally placed in the front part of the ornamental alcove, the 'tokonoma;' on rare occasions, by its side. There are many kinds of incense burners of rare and costly porcelains, pottery or bronze. The shapes fall under the classifications of legged type with suggested handles on each side, those resembling the head of a ceremonial water dipper, and those approaching miniature casks in form. Occasionally one sees an old incense burner of bronze but for dwarfed tree exhibitions porcelain is favored. To make the display of incense burners convincing, tokonomas are sometimes suggested at the shows.

Westerners, using whatever interesting objects they may have on hand as improvised incense burners, might add a new and exotic accent to their bonsai displays.

## 6.  VASES, STONES, SAND

Flower vases are used at such events, too, being arranged in harmony with the tree, with flowers tending to accentuate the colors of trees, pots and stands; but perhaps the most unusual and fascinating accessories are the strangely shaped stones of beautiful design and texture displayed in shallow trays of water or sand. These deserve the serious consideration of Westerners interested in artistic things. In some arrangement sands are spread and well selected stones and trees placed on these. The result is an actual landscape with a strong and convincing feeling of depth. Furthermore, the water stones make magnificent showings by themselves, at times suggesting distant mountains or cliffs and when correctly arranged in a tray, giving the impression of heroic natural scenes. Just as dwarfed trees bring out the characteristics of their various species to the greatest advantage, stone arrangements display the latent beauty of rocky landscapes in surprising reality. There is this added advantage: trees die and stones do not. If one tires of stones, it is a simple thing to put them away until again wanted. Natural stones are sometimes used as ornaments in the tokonoma the same as dwarfed trees. Carved and cut stones, leaving nothing to the imagination, are valueless. Needless to say, such things as patching with cement, etc., are out of the question. The more usual stone classifications are as follows:

1.  Far Mountain—with the shape of a wide-based triangle, resembling a mountain.
2.  Lone Island—resembling a detached mass of rock in the sea.
3.  Rocky Mountain—a steep, rocky peak.
4.  Cliff—precipitous, vertical stone.

Various stones used with dwarfed trees:

A.  Rounded bits of quartz from a Sierra mountain river.
B.  Angular, water-worn quartz.
C.  Various beautifully veined and layered stones from windy hilltops.

Water stones from the beach:

A.  White stones arranged against darker gravel.

B.  Chinese Juniper and handsome water stone, with
    colored gravel.

C.  Closer view of same.

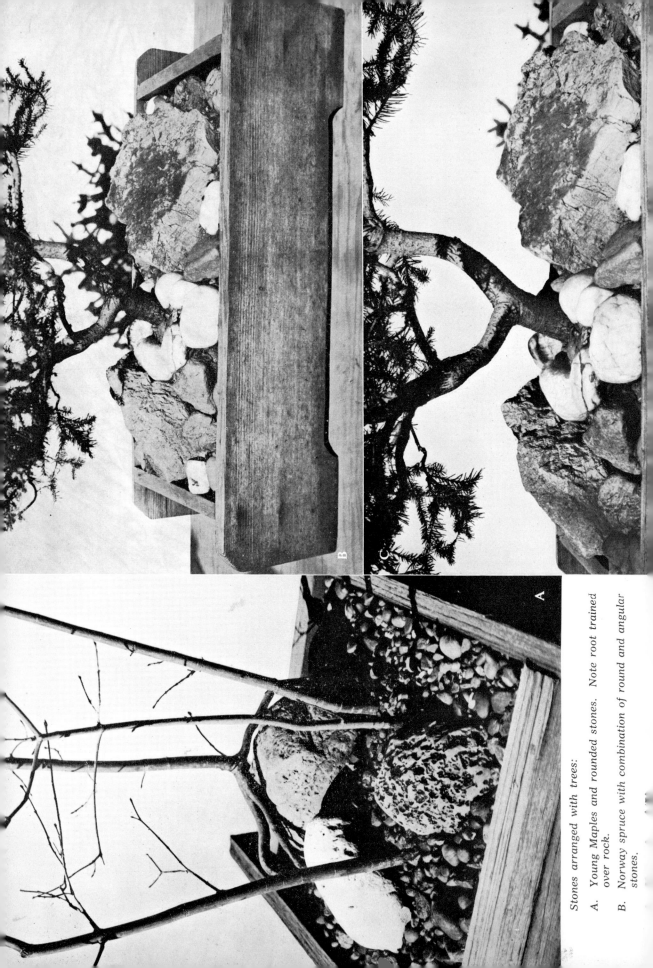

*Stones arranged with trees:*

A. Young Maples and rounded stones. Note root trained over rock.

B. Norway spruce with combination of round and angular stones.

*Stones arranged with trees:*

A. *Young Sargent's Juniper with serpentine and gravel.*

B. *Chamaecyparis elwoodi with well formed roots among mountain and beach stones.*

*Western arrangements of stones displayed in trays of sand, the shapes suggesting:*

A. Lone Island        C. Rocky Mountain (raked sand)
B. Cliff        D. Lone Island (sand raked in squared pattern)
E. Water Collecting (sand pattern conforming to shapes of stones)

5.  Great Waterfall—stone with veinings suggesting a waterfall.
6.  Earth Slope—gently sloping stones.
7.  Thatched Cottage—eroded stones resembling country cottages with thatched roofs. These, found only in a few places, are formed by a softer strata wearing away between two harder ones. Pieces ground to curves by water really do suggest the thatched farm houses of Japan.
8.  Water Collecting—stones with hollows of various shapes in which water stands.

In the Far Mountain and Steep Peak forms, stones are classified according to their folds and textures. One reads of "open linen folds," "wide folds" (narrow and deep crevises and cracks). Stones are also divided into the three classifications of formal, intermediate and informal, the same as gardens and calligraphy or flower arrangements.

Formal stones have the contours of steep mountains and great rocks.

Intermediate stones are more serene in shape.

Informal styles are the Water Collecting, Thatched Roof and Earth Slope styles.

The appreciation of these stones consists of arranging them in water trays and viewing them, but if coarse sand is also spread and moss planted, the effect is greatly enhanced. There are other ways of placing stones. Not only are they admired by themselves, but are combined with dwarfed trees as parts of the composition, and sometimes the trees themselves are planted on them. The usual method for this is to select a stone which harmonizes with the tree to be planted. Placing the stone to the left, in a pot filled with earth, turn it so the most interesting cracks and folds appear to the front, and firm it into place on the soil. After the cracks have been rammed full of earth the tree's roots are led over the stone and covered with moss, the ends of the roots reaching down into the pot. This method will be discussed in detail in Chapter 4.

There are many other ways of arranging stones. With straight-trunked trees and in similar instances, relatively flat stones are placed about the roots, or the stones shaped like thatched houses are set to suggest a remote country village. With such plants as dwarfed Bananas and dwarfed Bamboos standing stones are employed. With Grasses and plants of a perennial nature, the general rule is to use the water gathering stones. In placing flat or standing stones, the spirit of the Chinese school of painting is followed. Stones with interesting folds and textures are good. This technique is seen in pictures of Chinese gardens where full sized Bamboos are combined with huge vertical stones. The use of the thatched house stones with suitable trees is rather common.

## 7.   THE WESTERNER AND JAPANESE TRADITION

A Westerner taking up the hobby of dwarfed trees need not be bound by traditional approaches to the subject.   Trees can be trained with a freedom not seen in Japan, arrangements can be created to suit the spirit of the occasion and such accessories as tables, backgrounds, shelves and benches can be designed to harmonize with Western ideas.   An interesting aspect of Westernized dwarfed tree culture is the use of beautiful stones and pebbles around the tree trunks.   Some trees can even have their roots trained over stones. The colors of the stones bring out the contrasting greens of foliages and such things as worn pieces of quartz or jasper when used sparingly, add a bit of lightness not otherwise seen in dwarfed trees.   This again can be done to suit our individual tastes.

The searching for unusual specimens of driftwood and the using of these for accent pieces, or stands is another hobby easily combined with dwarfed tree growing.   Even a prosaic board when beaten by waves often assumes just the form needed for a low shelf on which to place a few trees.   Our mountains and seashores are wonderful hunting grounds for all sorts of things useful in the embellishing and displaying of bonsai.

The important consideration is the adding of something of ourselves to these combinations.   A mere copy of a photograph will never have the charm of a simple spontaneous arrangement reflecting the spirit and essence of the moment.   When we are finally able in our own way to suggest the beauty of a great tree within the limited dimensions of a pottery tray, the growing of dwarfed trees will have become a vital thing with much of its original Oriental significance.

The mere possession of a collection of well made dwarfed trees is, in itself a great satisfaction.   The caring of the differing varieties throughout the year, the seeing and being the cause of constantly increasing beauty, the showing of trees to interested friends, all are sources of unending pleasure.   There is a strong sense of having really accomplished something.   The years of one's labor have produced living things of beauty and value.

But this is not the ultimate goal.   There must be a definite and intimate connection between the dwarfed trees and one's daily living if we are to appreciate the fundamental spirit of nature that underlines the whole art of making miniature trees.   We of the West can easily accomplish this.

Trees can be kept in places where they are constantly seen and enjoyed. A special patio table artistically constructed will hold a tree or two.   An ornamental shelf against a bit of garden fence near a frequently used path is sometimes ideal.   The taking of trees into the living room for a day or so and then replacing them with others, provides a constant and ever changing panorama of the differing and more subtle aspects of favorite specimens.   Each dwarfed tree fancier can easily add to these ideas and create a method of his own for the displaying of his treasures, making the hobby of dwarfing trees an intimate part of his daily living.

There is no end to the ever-expanding activities connected with this wonderful hobby.

## 8.  MAME BONSAI

For example, the cultivation of Miniature Bonsai, called "Mame Bonsai" or "Bean Sized Dwarfed Trees," has become popular and opens up many new vistas. The Mame Bonsai are a real challenge. All the cultural directions applying to larger dwarfed trees are met with in an exaggerated form. The first rule—never let the plants dry out—is of course difficult to maintain as the pots are so tiny that the little trees must be watered several times a day in hot weather. The finding of specimens with good shapes and short needles or very small leaves is another problem. These difficulties act as a spur to the enthusiast who is justifiably entitled to a sense of accomplishment when he produces a two inch tree of excellent form.

As not many Mame Bonsai are found growing in nature, most are propagated from seed, sometimes started in the very pot the tree is to occupy in the future. More are the result of the selection of likely looking cuttings. If one roots cuttings with the beginnings of branches, it is not difficult to eventually have trees with most of the charm of those many times their size.

Strangely enough the Mame Bonsai are just as hardy as any dwarfed trees, and if properly cared for will live to ripe old ages, producing healthy foliages, or blossom and fruits, according to their differing varieties.

The assembling of a collection of Bonsai pots small enough for these miniature trees is a hobby in itself, with such things as toy porcelain bowls, rouge cups, salt dishes and so on, taking on a new lease of life when carefully drilled with holes so the plant will have necessary drainage. Of coure Japanese have pots available in all sizes, but half the fun is exploring the possibilities of one's own cupboard.

*Displaying "Mame Bonsai".*
*A stand about two and a half feet tall for displaying miniature dwarfed trees.*

*Dwarfed trees take time. Showing some Blue Lawson Cypresses from cutting to mature tree—a span of about ten years.*

*Chinese Juniper—A very handsome old specimen.*

# CHAPTER 2.

## Collection, Propagation and Training

### 1. NATURAL COLLECTION

A considerable portion of the famous dwarfed trees of Japan were originally taken from natural locations high in the mountains or along windswept cliffs. While the work of locating, moving and training of such trees is great, the results attained far exceed those of any other method, except of course time itself. This natural collection has always been the goal of dwarfed tree fanciers and all sorts of elaborate precautions have been devised for the safe transplanting of the trees.

Digging is done in mid-winter when the trees are dormant or just before the new growth appears in Spring. If trees are large some of the roots are trimmed a year before the final moving so the tree can send out small roots to compensate for the ones lost and in this way provide a mat of hair roots to be available after transplanting. Another method is to move the tree but immediately replant it in its native habitat, giving it a year to recover and then redigging and moving it to the nursery.

Tools for digging are knife, trowel, saw, spade and mattock. The ball of earth should be large and most roots should be saved, but seldom are these ideal conditions met. One usually ends with a bare rooted, badly damaged tree and the chances of saving it are correspondingly slight. However, if the roots are cut cleanly and the tree is kept moist at all times, there is hope for its living but after removal from the wilds one can expect to wait a good many years before it entirely recovers.

The moving of young trees is a much simpler job and the rate of loss considerably less. Young trees move readily, their roots are easily controlled and with a minimum of care most eventually make good, but not exceptional, dwarfed trees.

The difficulties being what they are and the sources of good natural trees becoming exhausted, most are now grown by other methods. Unless one is prepared to spend much time and money in the search, the chances are that the rewards of collecting from natural sources would be considerably less than the results obtained from buying nursery stock and training it.

From personal observation it has been found that there are some varieties of trees and shrubs that are fairly easy to move and train. Among these might be mentioned Junipers of all descriptions. There is no special difficulty with Junipers because their matted roots are easily dug. Another tree which readily takes to transplanting is the Lodgepole Pine *(Pinus Contorta)*, a native of the California Sierras. These make interesting windswept shapes and can be trained with most of their roots exposed over stones. The Monterey

Pine *(Pinus radiata)* is another but should be of fairly good size as it unfortunately has a poor shape when young.

Generally speaking the smaller needled evergreens transplant more readily than the long-needled kinds and the deciduous trees more readily than the broad leaved evergreens. Any person with experience in the growing of plants will soon sense which are worth trying. Occasionally the unpredictable happens and one has the pleasure of taking home a large and handsome tree with no apparent trouble at all. Hitting the right time, weather and circumstances one can sometimes do the impossible.

## 2.  GROWING FROM SEED

The growing of dwarfed trees from seed takes longer than other methods. But after four or five years, results begin to show and after that the trees rapidly develop. For growing excellent shapes and well formed roots, seeds are best, being vastly superior to grafts or cuttings. The shapes of seedlings are natural and the spread of the roots, the design of the trunk and the placement of the branches need little correcting.

The novice can develop relatively large plants from seed in about five years. The trees most usually planted are Plum, Maple, Ginko, Cherry and some Pines. An even easier method is to go into the fields and mountains, dig up small seedlings, place them in pots and train them.

Seeds are planted in various ways. Usually they are sown in flats or pots, or they can be planted in the ground itself. Small seeds are best cared for in pots. After the seedlings have sprouted they are given dilute liquid fertilizer to develop their strength. The first transplanting takes place the following Spring. At this time they are severely pruned; tap roots are drastically cut and trunks are trimmed to the desired length. A heavy cutting back determines the future shape of the tree.

If, over a period of four or five years, leaves and branches are properly trimmed, the young trees will be more or less completed. During this time all the characteristics of special shapes can be developed.

## 3.  GROWING FROM CUTTINGS

There are many trees and shrubs that easily root from cuttings and the varieties that do not grow well from seed and are otherwise difficult to increase, are likewise propagated from cuttings. These develop better than grafts. There is no worry about the root stock sending out sprouts and one can make many trees at a time. With the use of a modern hot frame and various rooting mediums the cuttings may be speedily rooted and some small trees produced in a single year. The growth is somewhat faster than that from seeds.

Cuttings may be taken at various times. In the case of plants that send out many sprouts such as the Flowering Quince, the middle of October or early Spring are both good. Most evergreens are trimmed in the Fall and if these trimmings are made into cuttings and put into flats they can be rooted by the following Spring. After the new growth has hardened, Summer cuttings are made and root faster than those from older wood.

The usual method of making cuttings is first to prepare some flats by filling them with coarse sharp sand or some prefer sand with a very small amount of earth mixed, as this fertile material seems to help in the development of roots. Sometimes a half inch of peat moss in the bottom of the flat aids in the distribution of moisture. The freshly trimmed cuttings are dipped in some rooting material, placed in rows about an inch apart in the flats and thoroughly soaked. Flats should be kept in a warm sheltered location out of the direct sunlight. If one wants to speed the process, an electric heating unit is installed under them which cuts down the time of rooting from one half to two thirds. However, the time of rooting is seldom a worry to the dwarfed tree grower as in a few years he usually has dozens of little trees awaiting training.

Trees grown from cuttings do not have as spectacular roots as those from seed. But the great virtue of cuttings is that variegated and otherwise differing varieties may be propagated true to form—an impossibility from seeds.

Always use sharp shears or knives in the making of cuttings. If the ends are cut diagonally and split, rooting will be speeded.

## 4. LAYERING

Some trees can be propagated by layering. This is valuable in the case of plants that have grown too tall and trees with badly formed roots.

The manner of layering differs but one general method is to select a branch of good form on some parent tree and, at the place where the cut is to be made, make a U-shaped incision cutting through the cambium layer. The bottom of the U is nearest to the ground. This cut is then filled with peat moss, kept moistened and tightly bound with twine. After being left for a period of several months, roots, begin to form. It works on this principle: Leaves suck up nourishment from the roots and in turn, return their contribution to the lower parts of the tree maintaining a constant circulation. If a U-shaped incision is made, the rising sap is not seriously affected but the returning juices are caught in the inside of the U with no outlet. Congestion takes place and the cambium layer sends roots into the peat moss. After these roots have grown and developed, the branch is capable of self support and may be cut from the parent tree and planted.

As one selects a good looking branch in the first place, layering results in a well balanced tree. It is only necessary to develop the proper root system.

The best time for layering is about April or May when the tree is growing vigorously.  After the branches are taken from the mother tree and planted in pots, keep them in the shade for a week or so.  Varieties that are slow in making roots should be planted directly in the earth.  They are buried a few inches deeper than usual and cuts made here and there through their cambium layers.  Many trees do not respond to layering so this method of propagation has a limited application.

## 5.  GROWING FROM GRAFTS

Grafting is used more in the cultivation of ordinary fruit trees and not so much in the shaping of the dwarfed ornamental kinds.  However, among the flowering dwarfed trees that depend upon blossoms for their chief attraction, grafting secures flowers of the desired types and colors.  This is commonly seen in the little Peach trees sold in Spring.  Most of them have three or more branches of blossoms, red, pink and white all grafted onto the trunk and nicely trained.  If grafting is resorted to, it is seldom that a good looking tree results.  Grafts leave scars, bulges and other evidences of their artificial nature.

The season for grafting is the same for all trees—early to late Spring. Grafting usually produces weaker growths as compared with that from cuttings. There is also the danger of the standard growing faster than the grafts.  The more usual varieties for grafting are Pear, Persimmon, Apple, Pomegranate and other fruit bearing kinds, but perhaps less generally known, such trees as the different Pine varieties, the small leafed Maples, the Ginkos and various trees that make colored foliages in Autumn, such as Plum, Cherry, Crabapple and other flowering varieties, have all been grafted since antiquity.

Ordinarily such things as cuttings from Plums and Maples do not make good roots so with these another form of grafting, that is, In-arching is used. Several two or three year old seedlings are planted around the root level of the parent tree, the bark on the mother tree is slit and the bark on the saplings is cut at a corresponding place and the two are bound together. They are then wrapped in moss, kept moist and, if possible, covered with earth.  If this is done in Spring, usually the top of the saplings can be cut off about the middle of Summer.  If no saplings are available, roots of the same variety as the mother tree can be used.  Japanese Maples, for instance respond readily to this treatment.  The method of grafting roots is just the same and quite important, as the beauty of the tree depends on its root form.

## 6. METHOD OF POTTING, POTTING EARTHS AND POST-POTTING CARE

Dwarfed trees limited to a small amount of earth, over a period of years, eventually send out quantities of roots which completely fill the pots. Drainage becomes impaired, fertilizer in the soil is used up and, if left in this condition the tree will slowly wither. The novice will suspect that other things are the matter but repotting is the general cure for ailing trees.

Evergreens are usually repotted from the end of February through March up to the Spring Equinox. Some Pine varieties can be repotted up to the first of May in colder climates. The time when new buds are just about to appear is best. If the Spring season for transplanting is missed, one can repot in October with no particular difficulty. Deciduous trees are also repotted around the Spring Equinox. Pomegranates are repotted somewhat later, but before they bud. The Spring blossoming varieties of Flowering Quince are repotted at the end of Spring while the Winter flowering kinds are repotted the middle of October. The time when the plants are just about to put forth new foliage, as with evergreens, is good. Also, if the Spring season is missed, they can, like evergreens, be attended to in October.

Now let's take a look at pots. No matter what kind they may be, water must not stand in them. Due to shrinkage in firing or other distortion, it frequently happens that the part of the bottom nearest the sides is lower than the portion immediately surrounding the drainage holes. Water never entirely drains but remains in a ring. If used in this condition, moisture

*Some common Western tools used by the author in the cultivation of dwarfed trees.*

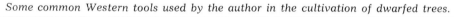

Repotting and trimming nursery stock.

A. Tree removed from can and roots being cut.

B. Materials used in repotting, including pot with drainage holes, potsherds, gravel, earth, ornamental stones, and tree.

C. The repotted and severely pruned tree arranged with ornamental stones. Very slow growing trees are pruned less drastically, but the shape of the trunk should be exposed.

B

C

Repotting a Deodar Cedar

A. Theoretical preparation of pot showing potsherds covering drain holes, gravel spread over bottom, and earth for planting. Other pots in rear show drain holes.

B. Tree in wooden container. New pot to right of tree.

C. Prying the matted roots from original container. (Continued on following pages.)

D. Cutting off surplus matted roots.

E. Final trimming of small roots.

F. Final trimming of large roots.

G. Pot being prepared. Holes covered with pot-sherds, bottom being covered with gravel.

H. Tree placed incorrectly in pot. Tree appears out of balance.

I. Tree correctly placed. Now in excellent balance with pot.

J. Completed tree, arranged with rocks and pebbles.

in the Ornamental Alcove of the Bonsai En.
In Chapter Three this same Cedar is shown displayed

collects and the roots of the plants commence to rot, so pots must be checked for drainage. Mix a handful of cement and fill all depressions so water will flow toward the drainage holes. Not much space is taken by the cement and there is no danger of destroying a serviceable pot. In very porous pots such precautions are not necessary as the water naturally seeps through the material. Common red clay pots can be used with most types of dwarfed trees, except at exhibition time, when they are replaced by more suitable containers.

Having chosen a pot with good drainage, let us proceed to the planting. Covers of some sort must be loosely placed over the drainage holes so earth will not be lost. Fragments of glass or small pieces of wood are not suitable as these materials have flat surfaces and sometimes stick to the pot and stop drainage. Pieces of earthen pots, or bits of crockery or broken shells are better as they have cracks and spaces that allow drainage. Some use bark from Palm trees or bits of wire screening. Materials of uneven surfaces are much better for this purpose than flat objects.

No matter what kinds of earths are used in potting dwarfed trees certain rules apply. Invariably, coarse material is placed in the bottoms of pots to aid drainage, even if the pots are large, or small, deep or shallow. This bottom layer is about half an inch thick and of bean-sized coarseness. Pea gravel is excellent and makes a fine base for the potting soil.

Certain trees prosper in certain kinds of soil. That is, one tree might like a preponderance of leaf mold, another ordinary fertile soil, or sand. Still others like heavy soils, and so on. Then there is the matter of packing the soil around the roots or leaving it loose. Pines do well if sandy loam is packed about their roots; other trees like different treatment. A safe rule is to try and duplicate the soils and conditions in which the trees are found in nature. If they are planted in a manner unsuited to their natural dispositions, best results will not be obtained. The earths used in potting and their proper preparation are more than half the battle.

There are various details about the level of the earth in pots. Sometimes the tendency is to have the earth rather low in the four corners and higher in the center or near the tree trunks. If this is done, the water is apt to run along the inside of the pot to the bottom to be discharged through the drainage holes without fully moistening the roots. There is the danger of the central portion being ever in need of moisture. The best solution is to make the four corners of the pot, or its circumference, and the center near the tree, high, leaving a valley between the two so water is trapped and must seep into the soil. By this method saturation or the proper degree of moisture can be easily regulated. Also there is the artistic effect. The slight curves of the earth help in the general beauty of the tree and the pot.

As bare earth is usually not expressive of the simplicity and beauty of nature, a layer of gravel and ornamental stones not only improves the general appearance but helps hold moisture.

Good potting soils have the quality of easy drying yet retain a certain degree of moisture. When potting, the earth should not be wet or, by the mere process of firming around the roots, it becomes like dough and water merely runs off its surface or gathers in puddles to rot the roots. It is best to have the earth slightly damp and then put it through a fine sieve. Discard the material that passes through the sieve and pot with the remainder, after coarser clods, sticks or other refuse have been picked out. Soils can be run through a coarse mesh for this latter purpose. In this way trees will be supplied with earth capable of holding sufficient water to throughly wet their roots while superfluous moisture drains away.

For about a week after potting until the roots again begin to grow, trees are not exposed to direct sun or wind but are kept in a protected place. It is an error to overwater after repotting with the idea of preventing the trees from drying. As the roots have been cut and their power of absorption diminished for the time being, no matter how much water is poured over them, it will have little effect. So watch newly potted trees carefully for a week or two and gradually, by degrees, bring them out into the sunshine to resume their usual existences but, of course, never let them dry out. If repotting has been well done, the tree quickly responds.

Earths in general use are: reddish subsoil (half sand and half clay), leaf mold, earth from fields and marshes, loam and sandy soils, and material containing peat. No matter what earth is used, the first rule, that of good drainage, is strictly adhered to. It is a common practice to include a good percentage of sand in most potting soils to assure this condition.

Experience has shown that a basic potting soil composed of five parts of loam, three parts of unscreened river gravel and sand, and one part of peat moss satisfies most requirements. This is an excellent formula for Westerners as all ingredients are readily available. Plants that have waited a long time for transplanting should have a larger percentage of loam added to the new soil. If leaf mold is available, this is even better. Pines, however, like a little more sand. As stated before, all materials used in transplanting should be only slightly moistened.

Sands are important. When soils are put through sieves and the coarser materials used, these particles eventually disintegrate, become solid and obstruct drainage. Here sand is invaluable as it permanently retains its texture. Sharp sands with angular particles are much better than those worn to round forms.

## 7. Wiring and Shaping

Well shaped natural forms of mature trees of the kind being trained are used as patterns, in growing dwarfed trees. Wires of sufficient strength to hold the branches in their desired shapes are used. Wires heavier than necessary

*Preliminary wiring of an Atlas Cedar, while still in nursery container.*

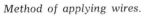

Method of applying wires.

A. Wisteria wired for bending.

B. and C. The finishing off of the upper ends of the wires.

D. Anchoring a wire at a crotch.

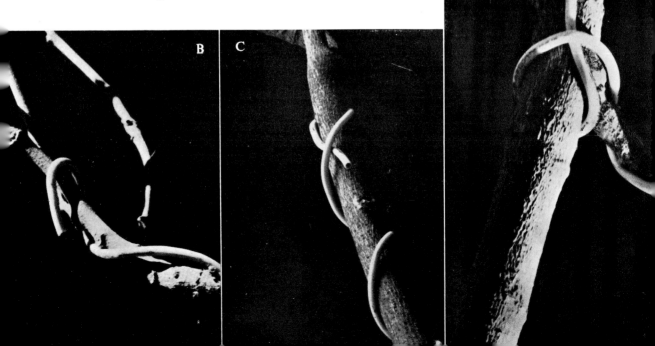

are to be avoided. Trunks are bent, branches are straightened or otherwise corrected and often trees are planted in groups and wired simultaneously. This is carried on at the season best suited to the nature and characteristics of the trees being treated, usually in early Spring. The wires should be of soft material and carefully wound, using the trunk as the base from which to work. Copper wire is generally used, applied with the correct degree of tightness. Wires are selected according to the size of the branch to be trained and are applied slowly and carefully, starting at the trunk and working outward. Soft, ungalvanized iron wire is also frequently used.

It is important to remember that some trees have exceedingly soft bark and all possible care must be taken not to cut this when applying wire.

The first turn of the wire, the foundation anchorage, is most important. Without being properly secured there is the danger of the wire suddenly loosening, and cutting the tree. First place the end of the wire across the main trunk of the tree, then pass the wire around the main stem, over the standing end and, at the same time around a branch (See Page 31). A firm start keeps the wire from slipping. If the tree divides into a Y, it is well to use one wire for both limbs, first passing it around the main stem, and, after crossing it, continuing out into the branches. This is not only more efficient but looks better. Always leave room for expansion, or the wires eventually cut into the bark and make unsightly marks. Also as copper wire sometimes becomes hot in the Summer heat, the branch held too tightly will swell out of proportion. If the tree is loosely wound so that the wire only touches at important points, just enough to maintain shape, there will be no injury. Some tree growers wire tightly for style and immediate appearance but it is not done by those really having the best interests of the trees at heart.

A peculiar point is that in trees wound too tightly the swellings on the bark occur above the windings while those below the trunks are smaller. The Japanese hold that the sap, returning to the roots, uses the outer part of the cambium layer on the downward trip and rises through deeper layers. Trees should be rewound at least every year and a half unless wires are not cutting into the bark.

Trees which break easily and limbs which must be bent at a severe angle are protected by the use of cloth or friction tape. The under layers are loosely applied and the final one put on tightly. Over these protecting materials the wires are wound as usual. The protected portion should be just a trifle longer than the area to be covered by wire but not too long as wires sometimes make the padding slip out of place.

There are trees and shrubs which would be injured by bare wire. In such instances, first wrap the wire in paper or use various sizes of insulated copper wire. The insulation not only covers the wire but protects against Summer burning and guards against copper poisoning. An even better method is to first wind all trunks and limbs with strips of paper and then apply bare wire but this is not at all good looking.

There are certain rules to follow in winding. When a branch is to be bent to the right, it is wound to the left, and vice versa. The effect of the wire is more and more strongly felt by the branch as it is bent so before the point of too great strain is reached, bending is stopped and the end of the wire pinched out of round to prevent unwinding.

Amateurs sometimes use wires entirely too heavy. At other times such persons will wind a limb, bend it to the left, find it uninteresting, bend it to the right, still find it uninteresting, then straighten it, and so on. Needless to say limbs cannot endure such treatment. Others let appearance and tightness obscure the fact that wire is used primarily for holding the tree in shape for its first years only and it is best to take things slowly rather than rushing the training and injuring the tree.

Carefully consider every turn of the wire before making it. Then, when each winding is finished, twist just a little tighter and bend the end so it will not unwind, putting the end of the wire under the standing part, in reverse of the beginning.

Some trees break easily. Trees which turn red with the frosts of Autumn, Persimmons and such, should never be wound when they are old. If it must be done, it takes a long time to train them. They are wound with comparatively heavy wire and every week or two given an added twist, gradually bringing branches into the required form.

As over half of the younger dwarfed trees have straight trunks, some method must be used to bend these. Naturally wire will not suffice, so small clamps are used. First wind the place to be bent with layers of hemp or tape, especially the outside portion of each bend. Then clamp a piece of heavy wood, cut to the desired shape against the trunk and exert pressure. A good idea is to line the wooden form with several layers of rubber (pieces of inner tube are excellent for the purpose, as these prevent injury to the trunk and cushion the form against the bark). In applying pressure through the clamp, work is stopped at the first hint of too much strain. After the plant has been left for a week or two, the clamp can be tightened. It is best to plant trees directly in the earth while this work is in progress rather than leaving them in pots.

April is a good month for such drastic treatment. Autumn is dangerous. Generally speaking the time of the rising sap is ideal but one must use judgement. Young trees will stand a lot more than old ones. The form used for shaping trunks should be left in place for a year and a half or two years. Some trees take even longer.

Dwarfed tree surgery has advanced greatly in recent years. Anciently there were but scissors, saws and straw ropes; now the use of wires, various ways of tightening with screw tools, to bend with, and a large assortment of other implements make the modern treatment of trees a severe and complicated process.

Naturally if one does not handle such tools with extreme care, there is always the danger of inflicting permanent wounds. If bark is unduly torn, surrounding areas may dry out and die as the tree can't absorb enough moisture to feed itself. The cambium layer takes a long time to grow and cover the damaged portion. Sometimes decay sets in and important limbs die and the tree's life is shortened.

Trees and plants being living things should be treated in the same manner as humans and, if it is necessary to operate upon them, the wounds should be smoothly trimmed with a sharp blade and if possible quickly covered with some type of air-excluding material. If this type of rough surgery is performed in the Spring, the cambium layer will send out new growth and within the year heal the trimmed places, making a trunk that looks quite old.

Shears are an absolute necessity. They are used in making and preserving the shapes of the trees. The dwarfed trees of the amateur immediately tell the experienced person whether he really understands the use of shears. If improper shears are used, the plant appears ragged and torn. Branches that should have been squarely cut, and tender twigs will both have broken ends.

There are certain defects in shears that cause these injuries. Shears with two cutting blades are the chief offenders. Western style pruning shears cutting from one blade only obviate this, although the Japanese use these in the cutting of fairly large branches only. In cutting smaller branches with the Japanese style of shears, the cut part should be painted with some preservative to stop drying. However, when tender sprouts are cut with rather dull shears there will be no great damage; but when roots are trimmed improperly the tree is injured. If the ends of roots are torn or damaged, they seldom heal; dirt enters, rot starts and eventually the root decays. If proper shears are used and proper pruning is done, the new roots, to quote one book "come out as thickly as a woman's hair."

When two bladed shears make a shearing sound when opened and closed, they are in excellent adjustment. Shears fall into two classes, those of heavy construction for cutting branches and roots and others of lighter, and longer design with thin blades for use in trimming foliage and soft twigs.

Different people like different sizes of shears so their hands can exert the necessary and correct pressures for good work. The length of the blade is a matter of personal taste. As not much force is used in the cutting of new sprouts, long and slender blades are convenient for reaching into the foliage. For leaf cutting and sprout trimming ordinary scissors can be substituted for the garden variety. Recently many new models of shears have appeared on the Japanese market but anciently there was only one type, called the "Nanban" shears, used by all gardeners. The tradition has it that these were originally imported from Holland. As the Dutch came up from the south they were called the "Southern (Nan) Barbarians (Ban)." Hence "Nanban" shears.

## 8. WATERING

In the care of a dwarfed tree watering is most important. Being planted in small containers there is the ever present danger or drying and once thoroughly dried, the tree is damaged. On the other hand trees with poor drainage may be seriously injured or even drowned by over watering. Again there are certain trees which like considerable water and others which prefer a drier soil. Then of course the seasons of the year and the temperature have much to do with daily variations in watering.

There are no hard and fast rules. The aim is to keep the potting soil in a fairly moist but not saturated condition. To accomplish this the potting soils are mixed with a percentage of sharp sand to insure good drainage. If the soil is not fairly uniform in texture, the top may appear dry while the bottom is saturated. More frequently the top appears wet and the bottom is dry. As one waters, the outer layer of soil is soaked but the inner parts and the bottom are not reached.

Knowledge of watering must be based on experience. By scratching or pressing with the fingertips, one can ascertain the condition of the soil. When fairly moist, it retains a certain amount of elasticity. If the soil has lost this spongy feeling and there are no signs of moisture, it is time for watering. A good test for the condition of the bottom soil is to take a small stick and poke it into the earth. If there is no moisture on the end of the stick, it indicates that the bottom of the pot has dried and one should water, but if the end of the stick is wet, there is no need for watering.

Trees such as Cryptomeria, Persimmons, etc., like plenty of water and for these there must be no interval of dryness.

From the Westerner's viewpoint the Japanese are overparticular about the water used on their dwarfed trees. River water, well water, rain water, water from ponds and tap water are all declared acceptable with the best being rain water. They hold that in falling it assumes the same temperature as the surrounding atmosphere and collects nutritive atomospheric elements, and if stored in a tank and the upper part dipped out and used on dwarfed trees, is about perfect. As for tap water and well water, these are not used directly but are first poured into a container and allowed to stand for some hours exposed to the sun to more closely adjust their temperatures to the atmosphere. These storage tubs are large enough to hold two daily waterings and are refilled every evening. If cold water is used they believe the growth of roots is somewhat slowed, and leaves are chilled. Depending on location there are parts of the dwarfed tree garden that require less water than others but even here the warmed water is carefully applied. Another virtue of this tub water according to the Japanese is that in time it fills with beneficial growth, especially if used with dilute fertilizers. Some Japanese use water from the bath or water to which bean cake has been added and this is excellent for watering dwarfed trees that have been planted in the earth.

There are various times for the watering of dwarfed trees but soil conditions are more important than set time intervals. Old time Japanese, apparently with nothing better to do, watered three times a day: morning, noon and evening. But for Westerners one good watering each day should be sufficient, except in the hottest weather. It goes without saying that watering depends upon the condition or degree of dryness, the daily weather and exceptional times of bright sunshine or strong winds. The largeness or smallness, deepness or shallowness of the pots, planting earth, kinds of plant material and certain characteristics of special plants make it necessary for one to investigate the dryness of each dwarfed tree and water accordingly.

The above lengthy directions hardly fit in with the busy lives of most Westerners, but do present ideas for consideration. However as stated above, a daily thorough watering with the hose should be ample, except in the hottest weather.

In the West where there is not the abundance of moisture found in Japan, the cultivation of healthy dwarfed trees will depend more upon the one item of watering than anything else. Well watered trees seldom become diseased. Lath houses with overhead systems of sprinkling to supplement hand watering should be ideal in the more arid sections. Through such labor saving techniques there is no reason why the daily care of dwarfed trees could not be made a comparatively easy project.

## 9. FERTILIZING

Various unfamiliar fertilizers are used by the Japanese. These range from soya bean cake to dried sardines, herrings and silkworm manure. Reliable substitutes available to Westerners are: animal manures, cow, sheep, etc., and the various fish emulsions now on the market. One rule applies to all. Use in moderation!

As to the commercial products such as sulphate of ammonia, etc., all of which contain a considerable proportion of nitrogen, they are never applied by themselves but are mixed with earth or other material to cut their strength. As they readily dissolve in water, a weak solution is given in early spring, when the plants are just beginning to bud. Late Spring is a period of little or no fertilizing. As the main new growth begins to harden, at that time plants are given a period of rest. Late Summer is another excellent time for applying fertilizer.

It must ever be kept in mind that the fertilizing of dwarfed trees is *not* done to produce new growth, except in rare instances. Fertilizers are used to maintain vigor and color and are purposely kept as weak as possible and given sparingly. If a dwarfed tree is over fertilized, the shape built up through the years is in danger of being lost under the new shoots. The labor involved

*Frequent and thorough washing of the under sides of foliage is the best insurance against insect pests.*

in maintaining the tree is doubled and the tree itself suffers considerably due to this increased pruning and wiring. Many trees require practically no fertilization whatsoever. A dilute application in early Spring and another in late Summer will be sufficient in the majority of cases. In a book of this sort the optimum care of trees is described but there are always short cuts available to the experienced gardener, and the Westerner would do well to underfertilize his trees.

## 10.   PESTS AND THEIR CONTROL

Dwarfed trees have their usual quota of insect pests but in addition to such expected things as ants and aphids, which can be controlled by a liberal spraying with the hose and by keeping the soil well watered, there is another disease that should be mentioned. Varieties of Pines, Cryptomerias, Junipers and other needle-bearing trees have branches turn brown and die. This is a form of red spider and is prevented by spraying the under and upper sides of the needles with water from the hose daily throughout the Summer. Most insects hide on the under sides of leaves and needles where the usual overhead spray has no particular effect upon them. When trees dry out in warm weather it is a direct invitation for such insects to attack. So keep the plants moist at all times. This is the easiest and surest method of insect control. If trees do not respond to such treatment, drainage and the necessity for repotting should be investigated. If these are in order and the tree still sulks, it is better to throw it out than waste time spraying and fussing with it. A healthy tree is a joy but a sick one is more trouble than it is worth.

In recent years entirely too much emphasis has been placed on the spraying with chemicals and combating of insects after damage has been done and too little on the keeping of plants in a condition where artificial aids to health are not needed. If dwarfed trees are properly attended to, they should not have to be sprayed with insecticides. Unfortunately this is sometimes impossible to avoid. In such cases the spray must be weakened to the point where it will not damage foliage or buds or coat the tree with an unsightly film.

## 11.   WINTER CARE AND PROTECTION

As dwarfed trees live in small pots they must not be allowed to freeze when cold weather comes. Although actual heat is not a necessity the pots and trees should be protected to the point where the pots will not be cracked or damaged or the trees injured. The simplest construction for such purposes would be a set of shelves facing South, covered with mats or awnings during freezing weather. But while this method is effective, there should also be some thought of appearance as one wants to look at his trees and enjoy them even at this season.  Some Japanese construct hothouses in Western style in which to store their trees; but if this is done, it must be remembered to keep the trees at a low temperature to prevent forced growth.  Dwarfed trees need a period of absolute rest.  The more usual construction, found in the homes of many Japanese dwarfed tree fanciers, is a sort of small lean-to made of window sash built along one side of the living room.  Between the living room and the trees is placed a partition of sliding glass doors.  In this way the trees are kept at any desired temperature and at night the glass doors can be opened slightly to allow heat from the house to neutralize the cold.  When the season for early flowering arrives, one needs but to open the doors and the entire house is perfumed by the fragrance of the blossoms.

Another simple way of maintaining sufficient warmth with this arrangement is to suspend a 40-watt electric light over the trees.  The globe maintains the temperature above freezing, provided the construction consists of but a couple of short shelves and is covered at night with mats on the outside.  Larger shelves would require more heat.

It is well to remember that if plants are placed in a hothouse for forcing without first being exposed to the Winter cold their blooming is irregular.  Better to expose them to one or two severe frosts and afterward bring them in.  At first they can be placed in a fairly dark location on the floor of the greenhouse and kept at a low temperature as it is important that they be exposed to heat and sunlight by degrees.  In greenhouses equipped with cold rooms the plants can be left on shelves under the benches as this stimulates a Winter growth of new roots.  After the roots have grown sufficiently, usually in a couple of weeks, the plants are placed on the upper benches.

## 12.   Moss

Smooth, velvet-like Moss, beautiful and damp is surely an attraction when seen on the surface of soil in pots.  If no Moss is allowed to grow with the trees the effect is sometimes incomplete.  Moss increases rapidly under the daily watering of the trees until the entire pot is soon covered with lush green that one hates to throw away but if it is not thinned from time to time, damage will result.

Taking off the Moss, one notices that under it the tree has not sent out roots, and vice versa; in places where there is no Moss, hair roots are seen to be thick.  The reason is that the soil under the Moss is always wet and cold so the growth of roots is discouraged.  Also as heavy fertilizing is avoided in dwarfed trees and only dilute liquid used, the chances are that the Moss absorbs most of this.  Again if the tree should dry, things are even worse, due to the lack of root development.  It is best to strip off all surplus Moss, leaving only tufts here and there where they contribute most to the general beauty of the dwarfed tree.

*Above—General view of a dwarfed tree farm at "Bonsai Machi" near Omiya, Japan.*

*Below—Interior view of a winter bonsai storage house at the same place.*

Rustic display shelves in the Western manner at the author's "Greenwood Tree".
Above—Showing grove of Japanese Maples in a hand made Redwood container. The
fence in the background is made of hundred year old Redwood palings.
Below—Another similar planting of Japanese Maples. These photos were taken in the
dormant season.

# SKETCH PLAN of DWARFED TREE GARDEN

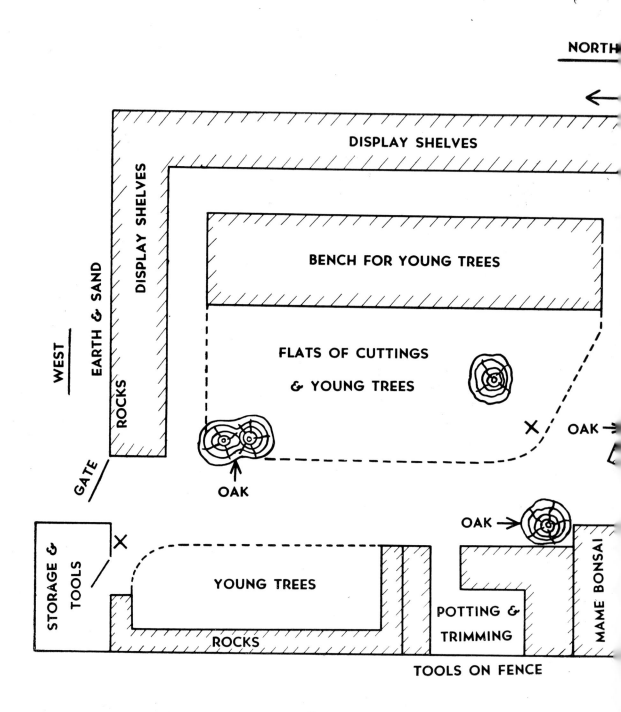

# AUTHOR'S BONSAI-EN—MILL VALLEY, CALIF.

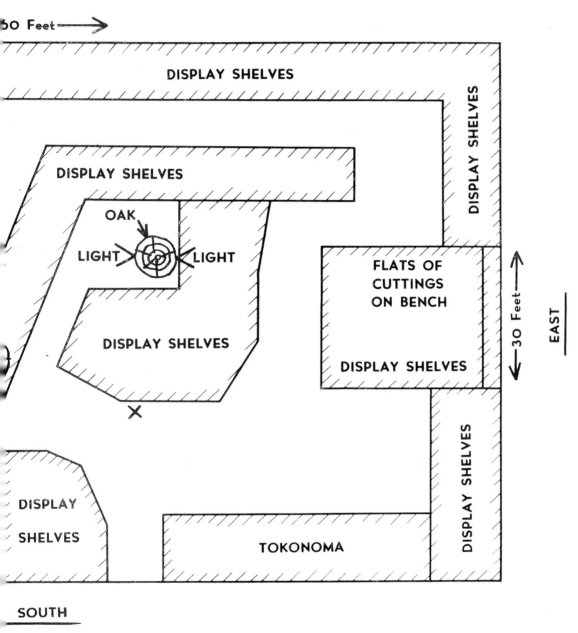

*Fences: Entrance to the dwarfed tree garden. A simple type of board fence, trimmed with Bamboo. (Bonsai En)*

*A good view of the workbench. Angular, weathered pieces of colorful chert are stored below. (Bonsai En)*

*Flats of cuttings: Prunings from various trees rooting in sharp white builder's sand. (Bonsai En)*

*Shelves for the display of rocks are an unusual feature of the dwarfed tree garden. The concealed door of the tool shed is beyond the coiled hose. (Bonsai En)*

*Above*—Dwarfed Trees placed in proper degree of sun and shade, and spaced to allow for growth.  *(Bonsai En)*

*Below*—Lath protection for the sunnier parts of the dwarfed tree garden.  *(Bonsai En)*

*Ornamental Alcove: Excellent for displaying special trees.*

A. *Deodar Cedar with Western painting.*

B. *Same with Japanese scroll.*

# CHAPTER 3.

## Construction of The Dwarfed Tree Garden

Before embarking upon the actual growing of dwarfed trees, proper facilities for their propagation, development, and display should first be constructed. Beginners will want something simple such as a corner of the garden fitted to take care of a dozen or so specimens. Others will be interested in more roomy constructions. But be they large or small, in laying out gardens for the dwarfing of trees, many things are to be considered. These points, when included in the garden design will help make their culture pleasurable by providing the proper facilities with which to work.

Some of the more important considerations in the construction of a dwarfed tree garden are:

1. Gradation from full sun to two-thirds shade.
2. A lath house, if no other shade available.
3. Protection from wind.
4. Plenty of outlets for watering.
5. Preparation of soil.
6. Propagation.
7. Potting and trimming.
8. Storage for tools and materials.
9. Winter storage.
10. Shelves for the display of the finished bonsai.
11. Ornamental shelves for the display of rocks.
12. A special tokonoma for displays with scrolls, etc.
13. Nighttime illumination.

Referring to the diagram of the author's dwarfed tree garden on pages 42-43 let us see how it meets the above requirements.

1. GRADATION FROM FULL SUN TO TWO-THIRDS SHADE. The West end of the garden is under Oak trees, thinned to admit the required amount of light. In this type of thinning, called 'daylighting' only the smaller branches are cut, preserving the beautiful outlines of the Oak trunks and branches. Daylighting is done every other year, but is not too expensive. A competent tree surgeon can thin a large tree in a few hours.

2. LATH HOUSE, IF NO OTHER SHADE IS AVAILABLE. Shown in the sunnier part, but not necessary over much of this garden because of the Oak trees. If a lath house is needed, make it large enough to give shelter not only to cuttings but to many of the trees. Roughly speaking, it would be well to have at least half the area under lath. One small section should have its laths spaced closer together to exclude two-thirds of the sunshine, providing an area for the care of newly repotted trees.

3.  PROTECTION FROM WIND. The entire garden is surrounded by fences. Most are six feet tall, except on the windy side where they are higher. An essential point is not to leave a space under the fence, as such an opening acts like a nozzle on a hose and directs a stream of cold air into the garden. If the fences are tightly made, a difference of ten degrees or more in warmth can be achieved. A second merit of this type of construction is the conservation of moisture. Drying winds are deflected and the dwarfed tree garden retains a pleasantly moist atmosphere. The design of the fences should vary in different parts of the garden. If there is an ornamental roof on one section, it should be omitted in another. Interesting patterns can be made by using the same kind of lumber but combining boards of differing widths, or alternating wide and narrow boards, or boards and grape stakes, and so on. Designs for fences are innumerable. However, the final result should be the creation of simple panels against which trees will show to their greatest advantage. No paint is used in the author's garden, the fences being of weathered redwood, but driftwood stain or something similar could be used to assure harmony between fence and trees.

4.  OUTLETS FOR WATERING ('X' on diagram). Nothing is more exasperating than a struggle with a long, kinky garden hose. The wise gardener sees to it that there are plenty of faucets in his dwarfed tree garden. They should be no more than twenty-five feet apart so a twenty-five foot hose will reach anywhere. Such an ideal condition has almost been reached in this plan but, although hoses reach, they don't seen to overlap quite enough. The hoses themselves need not be large or heavy. The lightest kind of a a rubber or plastic hose will do the trick, as most watering is done by hand and at low pressure. Where a sprinkler will be needed, for instance in the sunny section, a better quality hose can be left attached to a faucet. One can even set up hoses and sprinklers in advantageous spots and leave them, or better still ascertain where the permanent sprinklers should go and install them with pipe, eliminating the hoses except for occasional check watering. At any rate, be sure to have enough faucets whether using built-in sprinklers on not.

5.  PLACE FOR PREPARATION OF SOIL. "Earth and sand" on diagram. As can be seen, this is located outside the rear gate. Here are piles of various soils, manure and sand. By mixing, any desired result can be attained. The prepared soil is carried to the potting bench as needed. As this part of the set-up is outside, it does not interfere with the beauty of the garden.

6.  PLACE FOR PROPAGATION AND ROOTING OF CUTTINGS. "Flats of Cuttings and Young Trees" on diagram. Just an area without benches of any kind. Flats are filled with sand and cuttings, using the potting bench for a workroom, and then laid in rows in the shade of the Oak trees. By smoothing the earth so the flats are in contact with the ground at all

points, watering is simplified, and drying is considerably reduced. When the cuttings have rooted, the flats are returned, one by one, to the potting bench, and the rooted cuttings transplanted either into flats of earth, or if larger, into gallon cans two-thirds filled with good soil. The less earth used the better, as there will be less trouble later in accommodating the roots to the dwarfed tree containers. Flats of cuttings are also placed on convenient, shady benches. It is advisable to sprinkle one or two handfuls of gravel beneath each flat to prevent a stoppage of draining from too close contact with the shelf.

7. POTTING AND TRIMMING. This is a compact little area with a wooden floor and sturdy benches about thirty-six inches high. As it is in the shade of an Oak tree, it is a delightful place to work except on the coldest days. The space under the benches is used for the storage of stones. Prepared soil is not kept here in bins as that would mean double handling. Several wheelbarrow loads are from time to time piled on top of the bench, ready for use, which means only one moving: from mixing pile to potting bench. Nails driven into the fence hold an assortment of hand tools used in this area.

8. STORAGE OF TOOLS AND MATERIALS. It is a small enclosed area about six feet square and about that in height, roofed with any cheap material sufficiently tight to keep out the rain. Inside are crude shelves for flats, sprays, labels, tools such as rakes, brooms, hoes and the like. A wheelbarrow is an indispensable addition. The author uses a low-slung aluminum wheelbarrow, kept under one of the benches near the tool shed. A piece of wood under the rubber tire of the barrow keeps it from coming in contact with the earth. Bales of peat moss can be kept in the tool shed, but should be brought out, opened up and soaked before being used. Next to the tool shed but outside the garden fence is the place for the storage of sand and soil and surplus materials.

9. WINTER STORAGE. Some dwarfed trees turn a reddish bronze in Winter, and other varieties are rather tender. It is well to have a protected place where these can be kept from too much cold. Due to the mild climate in California such an area is not needed. Putting trees under a bench or on the ground is sufficient.

10. SHELVES FOR THE DISPLAY OF THE FINISHED BONSAI. Shown as "Display Shelves" in diagram. The most extensive item in the garden, ranging from full sun to all degrees of shade. They are of differing heights and widths, with an occasional narrow shelf above. In making display shelves, leave about half an inch between boards to ensure rapid drying after watering. If fences are built with their framework inside, the fence rails can be used as supports for the back edges of shelves. This type of construction strengthens both the fences and the shelves, and the fence rails can be installed at appropriate heights to aid in the building of shelving. Where the

ground slopes, shelves of differing heights slightly overlap, avoiding a too abrupt transition.

11. ORNAMENTAL SHELVES FOR THE DISPLAY OF ROCKS. These are designated by the word "rocks" on the diagram, being between the tool storage and potting and trimming section. These shelves were designed in a free manner, with contrasting heights and the introduction of vertical partitions here and there. They are strong enough to hold up quite a weight. On them are arranged stones of many classifications, picked up on numerous trips into near and far counties and states. There are beautifully weathered stones from mountains, rounded ones from rivers, pebbles and water stones from the seashore, and unusual specimens permanently kept for garden ornamentation. In maintaining this rather extensive display the qualities of individual stones are kept in mind, and as one works with a tree he instinctively remembers appropriate material to combine with it. One never has enough stones. Not only the type but also the color must harmonize with the tree, and this calls for enough of each kind to completely arrange several containers of differing designs.

In passing it may be added that the collecting of stones is in itself, one of the most fascinating of hobbies, and when one collects with a definite purpose, his pleasure is doubled. The world is rich in extraordinarily beautiful stones.

12. A SPECIAL TOKONOMA OR ORNAMENTAL ALCOVE. 'Tokonoma' on diagram. All Japanese homes have an ornamental alcove for the showing of paintings, works of art, flower arrangements and dwarfed trees. It is fun to add such a feature to the dwarfed tree garden. In it, fascinating displays can follow one after another, and on special occasions scroll paintings can be used with the trees in Oriental fashion. The tokonoma shown was constructed on the back of the garden house. The wall was covered with narrow strips of dark bamboo, against which almost anything stands out to good advantage. As it is eight feet tall, it affords ample room for paintings. The floor of the tokonoma is about six inches above earth.

13. NIGHT ILLUMINATION. "V" shaped marks on oak tree. The flood lighting of a portion of the garden is good, but another pair of lights should be added. Even in its present state over half of the area is well lighted and a joy to visit after dark when the imperfections of the trees diminish or disappear, and shadows add drama not present in daytime. The tokonoma should also be furnished with some sort of illumination.

From time to time other minor points will occur to the Bonsai enthusiast, but the above description of a dwarfed tree garden covers the main requirements. Don't forget that all can be managed in a much smaller space, and that the art of dwarfing trees if necessary, can be carried out on an old table when one knows his plants.

The Red Pine (above) has a beautiful and delicate pattern of needles and branches.
(Below) A Five-Needled Pine of excellent Twisted Trunk Style. Both bonsai photo-
graphed by the author at Mansei-in, Omiya, Japan, May 1963.

# CHAPTER 4.

## *Needle - Bearing Trees*

### 1. PRACTICAL IDEAS FOR COLLECTING AND POTTING

In the Orient the making of dwarfed trees has long been a well established industry. Oriental tree farms have many elegant, mature specimens originally grown from seed. Perhaps seventy-five or a hunded years have gone into the making of the more beautiful ones. This is a goal that we Westerners may some day hope to achieve, but for the present the better part of our time will be taken up with the training of whatever older specimens are available in this country and the employment of as many short cuts as possible in making passable dwarfed trees from more or less ordinary nursery stock. The growing of seedlings can be started as a side line and in time will assume its proportional importance, but for many years we must use other means to overcome the Oriental lead in the dwarfing of trees.

This being so, what are some of these short cuts? In most commercial nurseries there are many small older specimens of Pines, Cedars, Firs, Spruces, Cypresses and Junipers that are practically made to order for our experiments. By searching one can locate slow selling trees in gallon cans—trees that have been 'kicking around' for years because of their peculiar shapes, occasional dead branches, lack of foliage, slow growth, etc. It is these that develop interesting trunks and a resistance to misfortune that makes them flourish if given the least excuse for living. These trees can stand the removal of most of their roots and smaller branches and if adequately potted and watered will in a few years of good treatment, transform themselves into things of beauty. It must be admitted that bargains take a lot of time to locate but that is half the fun, and once found they prove most profitable. The author has been able to pick up many trees in this manner.

Another method is to buy nursery stock in its usual excellent and uninteresting condition and grow it on for a few years, training to the required forms. Such things as the fascinating *chamaecyparis obtusa* varieties or various kinds of miniature spruces are especially nice. If one buys older specimens of whatever is available, it doesn't take long to shape them sufficiently and by purchasing smaller trees in quantity one can conduct a sort of mass training that will yield excellent specimens in a reasonable span of years.

Buying from nurseries has so many advantages over field gathering that the latter should be considered only as a hobby. When a tree is bought from a nursery its root system its complete, it has accustomed itself to living in a small container and with the exception of the Pine tree which is somewhat difficult to handle, major surgery in both roots and top will not seriously weaken it. Also most have developed a mass of roots and not single tap roots, and these masses are far too large for the necessary support of the tree. This is especially true of pot-bound specimens, where it is possible to remove up to half of the roots and foliage without damage. In fact this radical pruning and replanting in new soil, followed by daily watering and controlled fertilization frequently gives the plants an entirely new lease on life.

Let us suppose that the start of a collection of evergreen dwarfed tree prospects has been made. Awaiting a favorable time of year for repotting, the trees are placed in congenial quarters and well cared for. Watering is important—the giving of some water each day will in itself work wonders with many bedraggled specimens. The spreading of a handful of peat moss around their bases will aid in the fight against dryness. If some plants have dead branches that are not ornamental, these may be removed, but it is better to leave the plants "as is" until they are placed in their new containers, as they assume an entirely different aspect when removed from the old rusty cans and at this stage the effects of pruning on future design are almost impossible to foresee.

What are the best times for repotting and drastic pruning? In California one can do this type of work from September until the new growth begins to show in Spring. Trees should not be repotted during the growing season of Spring to early Summer. In the East one could repot in late Fall, or early Spring before growth starts but the plants usually have to be protected from freezing. Cold weather not only tends to heave the plants out of their containers, but sometimes breaks the pots as well.

When the proper season arrives one proceeds with the repotting, pruning, wiring and training of the trees. The first job is their removal from the old containers. If trees are in cans it is advisable to have a pair of can cutting shears and make two cuts from top to bottom on opposite sides. Then by spreading the two halves apart, the plant and its roots can be removed in perfect condition.

WARNING—*Handle the cut cans carefully as the fresh edges are sharp and dangerous.*

As soon as a tree is removed from its container one determines the extent of the root system. If long neglected the roots usually fill the can until not much earth can be seen, but if the tree has only been planted for a few months there will be but a few roots visible. If the latter condition is true, handle the ball of earth carefully so as not to break it. Now, having selected the new container for the tree, measure its inside depth. This will roughly tell to what degree the ball of roots must be cut. In reducing the quantity of roots, first carefully pick and push away all earth covering them from above. This eliminates a considerable amount, especially from around the trunk. Then, using sharp pruning shears cleanly cut through the matted roots, leaving a shallow block of earth and roots which will more or less fit the container. Do not knock off all the earth. Some dwarfed tree fanciers have a variation on this, that is, they wash off all earth, trim the roots and repot; but if one leaves a compact chunk of undisturbed roots and earth the plant has a much better chance of immediately taking hold and sending out new growth.

Now temporarily place the tree with its trimmed roots in the container and see that there is enough room left for new earth all around the edges. Then remove the tree from the pot, cover the drain hole in the pot with a bit of curved potsherd, put in a shallow layer of new coarse soil and place the plant as wanted, firmly pressing the earth around the roots until the whole pot is almost filled. This pressing assures the proper contact of cut roots and soil and keeps the tree in the right position.

Next comes the pruning of the branches. Place the newly potted tree on some object that will bring it up to eye level. An upturned nail keg on the potting bench is about right. This gives the proper angle from which to consider the tree. Keeping its future shape in mind, take sharp shears or scissors and cut off all unwanted parts. The important thing is to preserve as much of the basic form of the tree as possible while removing approximately the SAME PROPORTION of foliage as roots. This balancing of top against bottom is the secret of the entire matter. The tree will look rather thin for some time following such drastic pruning but dwarfing is greatly speeded and by the following season the new foliage will have a fresh and pleasant appearance. Generally try to preserve foliage that grows in a horizontal manner, cutting off parts and bits that grow up or down. Of course, as explained in Chapter 2, one can salvage many doubtful branches by wiring. If repotting occurs in early Spring, this should be the next step. But extreme care should be taken and only the very basic wiring done. Then when the repotting, pruning and wiring have been completed, gravel and ornamental stones can be placed around the trunk of the tree and the surface of the earth decorated. If the repotting occurs in the Fall, an unfavorable time for wiring, leave the tree alone until a more suitable season so as not to run the risk of injuring the bark. If this is done the tree will have a chance of establishing itself in the container and will not be disturbed by the bending on of the wires. During this time it is well to see that the soil is moist but not wet. Once the repotting, pruning, etc., are completed, place the tree in a shady spot and soak thoroughly, gently pressing the wet earth and rocks against the roots. After leaving the tree in the shade for a week or ten days and lightly watering it daily, bring it into partial morning sunshine, gradually exposing it to normal conditions. A dilute liquid fertilizing will help to re-establish growth. This procedure is not too complicated and if the roots are at all times guarded against drying, is almost one hundred percent successful.

## 2.  PINE TREES—GENERAL SURVEY

In Japan the pine has always been called the king of trees. Its beautiful trunks and branches, artistic forms, brilliant dark green needles, effects under snow and masculine strength give it every right to this title. No wonder the Japanese Black Pine is the symbol of the samurai—the warrior.

The varieties chiefly used in dwarfing are three:

Black Pine (Kuromatsu) *Pinus Thunbergii, Parl.*
Red Pine (Akamatsu) *Pinus densiflora, Sieb. et Zucc.*
Five-Needled Pine (Goyomatsu) *Pinus Pentaphylla, Mayr.*

These have bark with divisions like the patterns on tortoise shells or designs resembling torn effects, that greatly add to their appearance of age. Sometimes such markings are likened to fissures in great stones, so these varieties are also known as Rock Pines or Brocade Pines.

Pines grown in pots are repotted once every three years, about the end of November. For the training of the trees into proper shapes, the usual wires are used. These are put on in January or thereabouts. If not attended to at that time, too much resin is liable to bleed, as it is almost certain that the trees will be nicked or slightly damaged in the process.

The new growth starts in early Spring but must be curbed to the point where the form of the tree is not injured. So it is cut back and watering is reduced to once a day to discourage the too vigorous sprouts. If the amount of water given is excessive the needles lengthen and the shape of the tree, built up so carefully over a period of time, is damaged.

If by error needles become too long, trimming is resorted to to preserve the proper proportion between trunk, branches and foliage. Branches that reach out from the inside of the tree or twigs that perform no particular functions are cut off; those allowed to remain have their needles greatly reduced in number and the new growth is trimmed severely. Fertilizers are not given until the new Spring growth has hardened which would be from early to middle Summer. The new growth is never forced.

There are many odd fertilizers used by the Japanese on Pine trees and most produce good results. Soy bean cake or dried cuttlefish juices are examples. For Westerners well diluted cow or horse manures or commercial fertilizers would be excellent. The point is to have the solution quite weak so as not to encourage extra growth.

The earth in which dwarfed Pine trees are potted is of the ordinary kind; that is, usually rich earth to which an equivalent amount of sharp sand has been added and well mixed. To one who has seen natural groves of Pines springing from light sandy soil, the wisdom of such a well drained mixture is apparent. Also it brings sharply to mind the necessity for constant attention both as to watering and fertilizing.

The Kuromatsu (Japanese Black Pine) *Pinus Thunbergii, Parl.* is inclined to bunch its needles together in tight masses when after a few years the soil in which it is planted becomes exhausted. When this condition occurs it is time to repot.

In order to help the formation of new places from which needles will sprout and the general character of the tree's growth over a period of years, it is well to water twice on very hot days. Even if it is Summer, trim off the too long needles to approximately one-third of their length; fertilize and new needles will soon make their appearance and restore the proper foliage effect.

The Goyomatsu (Five-Needled Pine) *Pinus pentaphylla, Mayr.* is especially suited to dwarfing. It has an exceedingly dainty habit of growth, small in all details with clusters of short needles grouped as in a Japanese print. The Korean Five-Needled Pine *(Pinus Korriensis, Sieb. Zucc.),* a close relative is rarely met with but is even more beautiful. Its special charm lies in the magnificent color of the trunk and limbs, imparting an extremely aged appearance. Its needles have a peculiar and beautiful lustre. This Pine has the happy quality of readily assuming the shapes of older trees, so its training is not difficult. It is truly a superior kind, most appealing when trained into the form of a tree springing from the face of a cliff, with long, down-sweeping branches.

The cultivation of the Five-Needled Pines is almost the same as that of the more usual kinds, the earth in which they are planted being but garden loam to which an equal amount of sharp sand has been added. Pieces of coke are placed in the bottoms of pots to make good drainage certain. Fertilizing material used by the Japanese are dried sardines and soy bean cake. The last is soaked and the liquid used. Again, Westerners would use fish emulsion or well diluted liquid manures. Trees are kept in locations where there is a good circulation of air and considerable sunshine, except in the afternoon. If the Winter season is not too severe it is not necessary to put them in cellars or beneath the eaves for protection but for the most part they can be left in the open. Wires for training limbs and trunks are applied in mid-winter. Most important is the caring for the tree's root system (drainage, etc.) and guarding against insects. Various scales seem to like Five-Needled Pines but they can be fought by washing the foliage frequently with the hose and by hand picking.

Pine trees planted on stones, must have good long roots. The Five-Needled Pine and others that have been cultivated in pots for five or six years without having their roots trimmed are good for this purpose. The long roots, circling round and round the inside of the pot are carefully loosened and straightened, and so made ready. Then these roots are led over selected stones and tied in place to keep the trees from moving in the slightest. Japanese use a cord made of palm fiber to tie the roots, but ordinary cord would be as good. The roots are carried along crevices in the stones, somewhat overlaced near the bottom and finally planted in the soil of the flat pot. The roots, reaching down the stones from all sides, meet beneath and embrace them securely. In this way there is no danger of the stones and roots separating at repotting time.

All portions of the exposed roots led over the stones are immediately plastered with a mixture of clay and peat. This not only helps to hold the roots in the positions wanted but protects against sunburn. It also adheres to the stones and does not easily wash off with ordinary watering or rains. Without it the roots would be in continued danger of drying before they had accustomed themselves to their new planting.

As Pine roots have many horizontal rings around their bark, it is necessary to use the utmost care in their handling. If broken at these places, the roots are either killed or severely injured. It is desirable that roots should not exactly follow the shapes of the stones, but occasionally stand out and away from them. This is artistic and has the practical point of avoiding any undue strain in straightening curved roots. Wire is not used to bind roots to stones. It eventually cuts, making permanent injuries and scars. As the roots, even after being securely tied in place, tend to resume their former shapes, the trees are constanly watched, bindings tightened, new daubs of clay added, and the whole kept constantly moist. The following year such struggles against a new way of life cease, and the roots can gradually be exposed to the air, and the bindings removed. When the rains come, let them by degrees wash off the muddy coverings, and the roots will harden sufficiently to begin the forming of a bark resembling the tree trunk itself. Strangely enough, trees planted on stones do not require as frequent repotting as those in ordinary pots. Five-Needled Pines so treated only need repotting once in every six to ten years. If moved too frequently the trees resent it.

For the beginner, it is easier and better to place the roots in their proper positions over the stones, bind them on and then bury roots, rock and all in the garden soil until well established, rather than leaving them in pots. The lower part of the trunk is also placed below the soil for added protection to the roots. The following year the plants may be dug and potted. After potting, the exposed roots are trimmed of all superfluous odds and ends and covered with the peat and clay mixture described above.

It takes considerable skill to plaster the roots closely to the stones; but once established the earth can be allowed to naturally fall away and eventually one has the roots only, with no earth at all, except at the bottom of the stones.

In planting trees on stones, place them in as contrasting positions as possible. There will be branches that look best when trained in certain directions; some stones will harmonize better than others; at all times, work for the attainment of a natural form. Trees with large trunks are unfit for rock planting. Trees in which the strength of the trunk is inferior to that of the branches, and trees with the first branch about as large as the trunk, can be planted on tall stones to make up for the lack of strength in their lower portions. Each should be considered on its own merits, and no forced effects striven for. Specimens with straight trunks can be grouped together on more or less flat rocks, like a grove of trees amid outcropping boulders on a mountainside. Such is the spirit of the art of dwarfing trees.

A little extra care is needed in looking after trees planted on stones. It is easy to water but half the pot, as the stone, being placed more or less in the middle of it, shields the rear portion from the sprinkling can. Trees should be watered from all four sides, and from overhead as well.

As trees planted on rocks are supposed to reflect their natural surroundings more than any other kind, one should always be one the alert to observe natural, large trees, on mountains or at the seashore, suitable for copying. On travels, this thought, if kept in mind and accompanied by a pad and pencil, could be the inspiration for many rough sketches of trees met along the way, one gradually learning to sense the spirit of attractive specimens and to impart the same feeling to his own dwarfed trees.

The exceptionally long roots one sometimes sees in photographs of certain kinds of dwarfed trees, and especially prominent in Pines, are not the result of natural growth. The training of trees in this fashion begins from the time they are seedlings, and one should be well grounded in the basic technique, as it is an amazing business, full of interesting possibilities. Examining trees as found in the hills and fields, generally the main or tap root is found to be the largest. It is surrounded by smaller roots reaching out in all directions and helping to nourish and support the tree in its upright position. In making dwarfed trees to represent such subjects as aged Pines springing from precipitous cliffs, where the roots run for distances over the exposed rock, the same natural effects of spreading support is essential. The goal is well worth the amount of effort required. There is nothing more beautiful in the world of dwarfed trees than the dark, glossy Pine needles contrasting with fissured rocks and gnarled and angled roots.

Here is the method: In early Spring, or Fall, the Pine nuts are planted. Eventually the seeds sprout, sending up miniature Pines which in time evolve into single, needle-covered twigs, about two to three inches in height. When the new needles on the end of this first year's growth are well opened, most of the center is pinched out, leaving only a few sets of needles. In the Fall the tree is dug and three quarters of the tap root is likewise cut off. This leaves several lateral roots.

The trimmed seedlings are planted in rows, in flats of good earth and sand. After a time, many new long and thin roots branch out in all directions from the cut off stub of the former main root. Ordinary Pines, having but one long main tap root are difficult to handle, as this root goes deeply into the soil; but if the tap root is severed at this early age the resulting second crop of roots is evenly distributed on all sides, and none will reach very far into the earth. This is a trade secret used by all dwarfed tree growers.

If the seedlings are given fertilizer, they will be ready for transplanting by the following Spring. At that time the roots are reduced in number to the required count, and all the little lateral roots, and feeders are removed, except at the root tips. Then, supported so that only the ends of the roots reach into the soil, the trees are planted. Roots are placed vertically, stretched into a straight line. The following year the tree is removed from the soil, the little side roots cut off down to the new tips, leaving only a bunch at the end of each root as before, and the tree replanted supported still further from the earth. As the years pass and this operation is repeated, the roots elongate with ever increasing rapidity. It is not unusual to have roots five or six feet long at the end of four or five years.

When repotting these specimens, support the trees with their shortened roots perfectly straight and hold up the longer ones by means of individual props, hoisting them to their ultimate length, otherwise the roots will sag toward the earth. The best tree for this work is the Red Pine (Akamatsu) *Pinus Thunbergii, Parl.* As seed from the Five-Needed Pines is hard to secure sometimes these are grafted on commoner kinds. Westerners could experiment with native Pine varieties.

Pine roots made in the above manner can be increased in length until they will be sufficiently long to suit any stone. Also Pines with most unusual trunks can be formed in this same fashion. Branches, of course, are trained in the ordinary way.

Some fanciers use another means for increasing the length of roots. Pieces of bamboo about an inch in diameter are filled with sand and soil, their lower ends inserted either in the ground or in pots of earth, and Pine trees are planted in their upper ends. The roots follow down the bamboo in search of better soil and more moisture. However, the length of bamboo which can be used in this method has its limits and longer roots can not be produced. There is one advantage: the tree is more easily supported. Also there is perhaps less tendency for the roots to dry. The bamboos are first split lengthwise then tied together and filled with earth. After the roots have grown, the bamboos are merely untied and there is no damage to even the smallest roots.

## 3. BLACK PINES
### (Kuromatsu) *Pinus Thunbergii, Parl.*

The Black Pine has always been considered by the Japanese to be supreme among trees. The needles are strong and robust, its shape is angular with interesting branches and bark patterns and dark green color. It is vigorous, and found in spectacular places such as cliffs, wedged between rocks, overhanging the sea or growing in groves from what appears to be nothing but pure sand. It is closely related in appearance to the Bishop Pine (*Pinus muricata D. Don*) the variety found in limited areas of California.

Dwarfed Pines are usually grown from seed or dug from the mountains. Although the usual Black Pine makes good dwarfed trees the Japanese have a special variety called the Brocade Pine (Nishiki Matsu) which has a remarkably irregular and rough bark. Being rare it is sometimes grafted onto the usual Black Pine. The shapes most suitable for Black Pines are Twisted Trunks, Half Falling Cliff Style and Full Falling Cliff Style. Aso they can be planted with Roots Clasping Stones or Groupings. The pots used for the Cliff Styles are tall in shape and those for the Groupings are flat and wide.

Trimming the Black Pine is rather troublesome. If the branches have become too long at the time of the tree's greatest growth which would be about the latter part of May, pick off all the new sprouts. Soon, from the bases of the last years' needles many new sprouts will appear. These future branches can be pinched back to suit. Repotting is best done in the Spring, usually around the time of the Vernal Equinox in colder countries, or before new growth starts. Black Pines can be left for five years without repotting but if the trees are neglected too long roots fill the container and the tree turns a sickly color. When this happens repot immediately. There are many twists and turns to Pine roots and they show ringed-shaped cracks. For this reason be careful when removing the old earth lest the roots break.

The soil used for repotting the Black Pines is usually about fifty percent sand and fifty percent good earth. The high percentage of sand insures good drainage.

Wiring is done in January before the sap begins to flow. In applying the wires be careful not to pinch the bark but leave room for the plant to expand.

A good location for Black Pines is one with considerable sunshine and excellent ventilation. A shady, airless place is an invitation for insects, the needles become weak and lower branches die.

Fertilize sparingly. Liquid fertilizer (dilute manures or fish emulsion) applied twice a year is sufficient. Autumn is good as it builds up the tree's strength for the coming year. Watering is done in the morning and in the evening. Be sure to spray the foliage.

The Bishop Pine *(Pinus muricata D. Don)* would be a good substitute for the Japanese Black Pine if the latter were not available. Native to small areas of California and closely resembling the Japanese variety, its care and training would be almost identical, as it is has great vigor and a good color and fairly rapid growth in its smaller sizes, it soon assumes natural shapes of interest to the dwarfed tree growers.

The Mugho Pine *(Pinus mughus compacta)* is another kind that is very easily trained to dwarfed tree shapes. Perhaps, of all the Pines this is the one the amateur should first try. Cultivate same as Japanese Black Pine.

*A truly remarkable specimen of Black Pine at Mansei-in, May 1963.*

## 4.  JAPANESE RED PINE

### (Akamatsu) *Pinus densiflora, Sieb. et Zucc.*

In contrast to the Black Pine the Red Pine is considered feminine as the whole nature of the tree is softer.  The Black Pines can stand the salt of the sea coast but the Red Pines cannot.  They are found inland or in sheltered locations. As they like dryness they prefer sloping situations rather than level areas. The trees have a reddish tinge and their special points lie in the smoothness of the reddish trunks with an interesting pattern of the bark and the tendency of the branches to sweep downward in natural shapes of good design.  The finished trees look like illustrations in color prints.  The needles are more slender than those of the Black Pine and are clear green.  Branches are rather thin.  In late Autumn the dead needles show, giving the trees somewhat the appearance of the Tamarack.

The following points should be kept in mind when making dwarfed trees of the Red Pines: They are the most delicate of all the Pine trees.  They are interesting and good but difficult to handle; the branches are inclined to grow too long.

Most Red Pines are started from seed but as it takes some time to produce interesting trunks these trees usually have little value until old.  They are trained in several styles such as Straight Trunks, Hanging Cliff Style, Half Cliff Style, in Groupings and with their Roots Clasping Stones.  As the trees are admired the whole four seasons, the Red Pines are a valuable addition to the dwarfed tree world.

The pots should harmonize well with the bark and needles.  For this reason glazed containers and those of white or yellow shades are not used. There must be plenty of holes for drainage.

Red Pines can be repotted in November or during the months of March and April in cold climates, earlier in California.  Spring is safer.  After transplanting leave the roots alone for five or six years.  In repotting disturb the tree as little as possible but cut away a couple of inches of earth and the wound roots from the edges of the pot.  Be sure to replace the coarser layer of soil in the bottom of the container and above it fill in with a small amount of fertile earth to which some sand has been added.  Check drainage at all times.  Use a piece of half inch Bamboo or stick and tamp the earth around the exposed roots, firming it gently.  Smooth the surface and water the tree sufficiently.

Wiring is done in January or midwinter.

As the Red Pine is a sun loving tree, keep it in an open situation protected from the wind and occasionally turn it around.

After repotting, give a minimum of water.  Weak trees are benefitted by having their pots buried an inch deep in the field for about a month.  This does away with worries about the proper degree of moisture.  Guard against too much drying in Winter and when the time for new growth comes, water moderately. Generally once a day in Spring and Autumn is sufficient, but during the hot Summer season water more frequently, and every other day in Winter.

Fertilizer is hardly ever needed, as it makes the needles grow too long. However, if the color of the tree needs improving, give two applications of very dilute liquid fertilizer about two weeks apart. It the needles start growing, stop fertilizing. Never fertilize until the new growth has reached full development.

Measuring worms and caterpillars are occasionally found on these trees but can be eliminated by spraying.

### SPECIAL NOTES ON THE CARE OF RED PINES

The main difficulty of the Red Pine is its inclination to make long thin branches, which are easily broken. Strong trees send out far too many branches which should be thinned to two or three. When the new growth has hardened the off-colored needles of the previous year regain their green color. Any that are unsightly should be removed together with those needles that are old and weak. This is usually around the end of September. One must wait until the needles have hardened before removing the unsightly ones, otherwise the new needles will be damaged. If the tree is subjected to heavy rain or strong wind immediately after having had its needles plucked it will be injured. In this case there may have to be a general evening up of the needles.

In wiring use wires in proportion to the trunk or limbs. On thin branches first wind the wire with paper. On thick trunks heavy iron wire can be used as forms. Sometimes the largest trunks are split on four sides with a chisel to aid bending. They are then wrapped in some protecting material before putting on wire, etc. This preserves the tree and aids in healing. Wires are left on for a year or two, but if left too long marks will be made which are a permanent disfigurement.

Don't keep Red Pines indoors for any length of time when the needles are growing. Also don't keep them indoors too long in Winter.

### 5.   JAPANESE FIVE-NEEDLED PINE
#### (Goyomatsu) *Pinus pentaphylla, Mayr. Pinus parviflora*

As their name signifies these are the Pines whose needles occur in bundles of five. Differing from either the Red or Black Pines they are native to high mountains and as their collecting and transplanting is quite difficult trees of distinction are rare. Sometimes the Five-Needled Pines are grafted on Black Pine bases but these are seldom outstandingly successful. The Five-Needled Pine lends itself to almost any shape, and being exceptionally robust looks

A. Five-Needled Pine with several trunks

B. This Five-Needled Pine is wonderfully preserved. The curving branches are a perfect design.

well with its roots trained over stones. The needles and branches are truly beautiful. The trunks have a good color, while the bark is rough and of excellent quality. Above all other Pines it is capable of making interesting roots so the Raft Style in which several trees are planted closely together, their intertwining roots eventually forming a sort of raft, can be used.

Pots are selected according to the shape of the tree, but the rectangular and elliptical ones are preferred. If the Five-Needled Pines have large trunks they can be trained as Twisted Trunks, Straight Trunks, Half Falling Cliff Style, and Full Falling Cliff Style. Differing from the Red and Black Pines, the large group Plantings of the Five-Needled Pines are hard to combine. So the Raft Style and the style in which two or three trees seem to spring from a single stump are more suitable. When trained over rocks the Five-Needled Pines seem to extend beyond the container, suggesting scenes of great feeling and depth.

As the Five-Needled Pines are among the strongest of the dwarfed trees they live longer than most and even if somewhat neglected still maintain good shapes. One can easily let them go five years before repotting.

Potting earth is composed of three parts river sand, two parts loam and five parts of sifted sandy clay, from which the finer bits have been discarded. This allows considerable moisture to be retained but does not interfere with the drainage.

Repotting time is March through April (earlier in California) or the latter part of September to the middle of October.

Wiring presents no troubles as the Five-Needled Pines are most pliable, but the branches expand rapidly and the wires should be removed each year to prevent cutting, and then re-applied.

Fertilizing, watering and location are the same as for the Red or Black Pines. However as the Five-Needled Pine has short needles only, it must be put under lath in the heat of Summer. Be sure to give as much water as for the Black Pines.

Diseases are the same as for the other Pines and appear mostly in Summer. Frequent washing of foliage in dry weather will keep the trees healthy.

Be careful about the pinching back of the new sprouts. As they are much less robust than the Black Pine one must use caution. Wait until the new twigs are almost fully developed and then regulate their growth to the length desired. If the tree is not too strong one can skip sprout pinching for a year.

## 6.   JUNIPERS—GENERAL SURVEY

The contemporary Occidental garden relies heavily upon Junipers for permanent plantings. The vertical kinds are popular for accent and those growing horizontally are used for massed effects. There are dozens of varieties of Junipers, some clinging tighly to the ground and others growing like Italian Cypresses.

Among these the Chinese Juniper (*Juniperus chinensis*) in its many forms is the most popular for dwarfing. It has ideal characteristics for all types of training. Having a mass of roots it can be moved without damage, its shapes are generally artistic and need but moderate correcting, the foliages of the different varieties are solid, yet not too heavy, and all are well bunched, so that the effect of a large tree is easily imitated. The Chinese Juniper is found in a number of variations. There is the plain green kind, solid and unchanging the entire year, and the variegated colorful varieties with silver or gold tips, especially charming in the dark Winter months. The Gold Tipped Juniper is a little slower in growth and should not be trimmed too severely as it takes time to recover, but the others can be thinned to any extent necessary to compensate for the drastic root pruning accompanying the initial removal from nursery pot and planting in the bonsai container.

The trunks of the Junipers are especially good from the viewpoint of dwarfing as they twist and turn and rather early in life develop a bark with shaggy scales. The roots too, when planted partly exposed, grow a bark of their own adding greatly to the age and beauty of the tree.

As to the shapes, those that thrust upward with long straight trunks can be made into unusual trees; those that bend over as if growing from cliffs and steep places are also suitable. When planted in groups Junipers soon adjust themselves to their new conditions, and specimens trained on stones do well. In making tree shapes they can be solemn or windblown, or pleasantly curved with sweeping branches. As has been stated before, cultivation is easy and they readily accommodate themselves to the fancier's ideas.

Considering the care of Junipers, a wide range of treatment seems to produce equally good results. Quite a number of growers are of the opinion that fertilizing is to be avoided, it being better to plant the Junipers in good earth and let it go at that. But there is no reason why a limited amount of liquid fertilizer couldn't be given, or better still, the mixing of a small amount of manure with the soil at planting time would aid the tree in its new growth. After one has worked with the Junipers for a year or so he will know the right amounts to supply. The Japanese prepare their repotting soil some time in advance, mixing the soil and fertilizer and storing out of the wet. The soil is finally powdered and used dry. Possibly a better idea is to slightly moisten the soil at potting time so it can be pressed into place around the roots. That seems to give excellent results and is easier as the pressed soil holds the tree in place as the work progresses.

In watering Junipers, once a day is usually sufficient. As in the case of all dwarfed trees, be certain to water from both sides of the container to assure a thorough distribution of moisture, and liberally sprinkle the foliage. Occasionally squirt water upward with considerable force, cleaning the under sides

*A young specimen of Juniperus rigida trained vertically.*

of the branches and tufts of foliage. This is important for all varieties and is the most reliable method for controlling insect pests. Needle-bearing dwarfed trees enjoy such attention.

Junipers take considerable sun but protect them from the drying western afternoon glare. This of course applies to all dwarfed trees.

There are no special rules for transplanting except as before noted; the foliage should be thinned in proportion to the amount of roots removed. The Junipers grow with enthusiasm and require a considerable amount of trimming anyway, so an added occasional cutting won't harm them.

Generally speaking, in the field of tree dwarfing, there are no more popular plants than the Junipers. Almost anything can be done with them and they soon take on great beauty with their lustrous foliages and handsome curves.

The Orientals have the saying 'Pines and Junipers for perpetual youth'.

The varieties of Junipers are easily propagated by means of cuttings. It is not even necessary to have a greenhouse to secure good results. Just take branch ends up to six inches in length, dip in a rooting medium and set in flats of moist sharp sand. Place the flats in the shade, keep wet and in a few months most of the cuttings will have rooted. If the process must be speeded, a greenhouse with bottom heat will work beautifully. Late Autumn is the best season, before the frosts begin. If the dwarfed tree enthusiast occasionally makes a flat or two of assorted cuttings, he will find that the natural, outside method of rooting will keep him busy enough. He is working with interesting shrubs and trees and generally can't resist the impulse to make far too many.

*Juniper—perhaps in time the West may approach such effects as this old Japanese masterpiece.*

*Above—Sargent's Juniper.   Three small specimens with interesting shapes.*

*Below—A whole grove of Sargent's Juniper.*

## 7. CHINESE JUNIPERS

(Shimpaku—Byakushin—Ibuki) *Juniperus chinensis-var. procumbens, etc.*

There are many varieties of the Chinese Juniper. Some have dark green foliages while others have gold or silver tips. They are native to China and much of Japan. Their special charm lies in their magnificent shapes and arrangement of foliage. In making dwarfed trees their growth can be controlled to any desired direction or design and the trees quickly take on an old and interesting pattern. Junipers have differing forms. Some are perfectly erect and others hug the earth in a flat mat. Those used as dwarfed trees usually have foliages resembling the Cryptomeria. Junipers have two types of foliage, frequently seen on the same plant. They are called:

CRYPTOMERIA NEEDLED (Ibuki) the spike-like form found on younger plants.

ROUNDED NEEDLED (Byakushin) the mature foliage found on older specimens.

The Japanese do not like the mixed foliages and the type not wanted is removed, but as the foliage is naturally inclined to become more and more rounded and of the mature type with the passing years, it is well not to pick off the Ibuki type too soon. Completed Junipers are very valuable. Some of the more famous were found in the mountains and made into dwarfed trees but by far the greater number are made from cuttings selected from trees with foliage of good form and color. As time goes on Junipers develop good form and beautiful exposed roots.

Cuttings are selected from trees with mature foliage. These are put in flats of sand and rooted without difficulty. Cuttings can be made almost the entire year but April or May and again September and October are the better months. Cut them cleanly with a knife, set them an inch or two into the sand, at an angle, and place the flats in the shade out of the wind. They root in a few months when they can be moved into the sun and given dilute fertilizer. Cuttings develop into nice little trees in about three years.

The foliage of the Junipers grows somewhat like the three-toed foot of a bird, and one always cuts back the middle toe to keep the branch from growing too long. The remaining side shoots soon develop and again one cuts out the center, gradually building up beautiful flat hands of foliage. The foliage should be trimmed while still soft but if it has hardened, shears can be used. Picking by hand eliminates the black ends caused by cutting with shears and encourages the foliage to mass into excellent shapes.

Although Junipers make berries, these reduce the strength of the tree and should be picked off while small.

Potting is done every two or three years. There is no need to do it every year. The best time is around February or March when the new color is beginning to show. Carefully remove the old earth with a bit of stick, taking care not to hurt the roots. If any of the original earth from the first transplanting remains, do not take it all off. Trim the small roots sufficiently but do not cut the larger ones.

In potting first cover the bottom of the pot with coarse gravel, then larger parts of clay well mixed with river sand so the pot will easily drain. Place the Juniper roots on this and complete the planting with a soil composed of six parts of black loam and four parts of sand. Do not use too much loam because the color of the plant is improved at the expense of good drainage and the latter must never be neglected.

After repotting do not overwater but do not let the roots dry. Place in the shade for about a week and gradually bring back into the sun. Be sure to sprinkle the tops. As the Junipers in their native habitat receive a lot of dew and mist, they are used to absorbing moisture through their foliage.

Keep in a place with a good circulation of air, morning sun and afternoon half shade. As usual protect from late afternoon glare as it damages the color of the foliage. Junipers don't mind cold but it is wise to guard against the roots freezing. Put them in a cold frame or some such protected place. Water occasionally to prevent drying. Winter fertilization is not necessary.

Fertilizer is applied in Spring when the foliage starts to grow. Liquid manure is used. Fish fertilizer will increase the luster of the foliage. One or two dilute applications should be sufficient.

Aphids sometimes attack the new growth and weaken the tree. In smoggy locations soot sticks to the foliage and has to be washed off.

The best seasons for the Chinese Junipers are Winter and early Spring. If put outside in January, they will turn red from the cold. To guard against this, keep them in a cold frame or bring them in the house for display. Later some exposure to cold will have good effect, retarding their too early growth. When May or June arrives most evergreens sprout new foliage and tend to obscure their shapes but Junipers do not, so can be on display the entire four seasons.

## 8.  Sargent's Juniper

### *Juniperus chinensis sargenti*

This variety of the Chinese Juniper has been grown in America for over fifty years. It was first introduced into the Arnold Arboretum from Japan by Professor Sargent in 1892. It is hardy and has tiny and beautiful needles, those of the mature plants being extremely dense forming attractive mounds and tufts of deep green to blue green.

The Sargent's Juniper easily conforms to those twisting shapes associated with dwarfed trees, such as the Half Cliff Style, Cliff Hanging Style, and so on. In addition the straight trunk style has a compactness that is ideal, the finished straight-trunked trees looking exactly like full sized specimens growing alone on some mountain slope. As this Juniper is easily trained and propagated and as the finished results are almost uniformly good, it is strongly recommended as a subject for the dwarfed tree fancier.

The care of the Sargent's Juniper is the same as for others of the *Juniperus Chinensis*. There is possibly one exception: the potting soil should be on the lean side, about half sandy clay, well screened, the finer portions discarded, and fifty percent rather poor soil with some sand added would be satisfactory. This assures good drainage and keeps the trees from growing too quickly.

## 9.   JUNIPERUS RIGIDA

### (Tosho—Muro—Muromatsu—Nezu)

Needles of this variety are narrow and sharply pointed. They remain on the tree for three years, are strong and sprout in great abundance, so that old and new needles are sometimes mixed, especially on the ends of branches. These Junipers are frequently planted in groupings. Single large specimens are rare as their shapes are inclined to be stiff. While they do not have the qualities of the Chinese Junipers or the Cryptomerias, they do have great vigor, and, more important, can stand being indoors for a time without the foliage becoming too long, so are used for Winter decoration in the house and for very small dwarfed trees.

Propagation of the *Juniperus rigida* is from cuttings and is about the same as for other Junipers. Potting soil is composed of seven parts of garden soil sifted and finer parts discarded, well mixed with three parts of river sand.

When planting the Straight Trunk Style use pots of a broad and wide nature. For Hanging Cliff Style tall and somewhat narrow pots are good. Earth colored containers are best as they harmonize with the nature of the plants. Always take special care to maintain proper drainage.

Repotting is done in January or February. The trees are then put in a location with no wind and kept under a cover of lath and well watered to help start new roots. After growth begins they are brought in the sun and fertilized once or twice with dilute liquid manure. They can stand a little more fertilizing than the average.

These Junipers need considerable watering. In Summer this should be done in the morning. In Autumn and Winter give whatever moisture is needed in the middle of the day. A sooty atmosphere soon weakens the foliage. Wash the needles frequently.

Wiring takes place in the middle of Winter. The usual technique is followed in bending branches and trunks. At other seasons the trees are rather brittle and cannot stand bending.

About March or April bunches of needles appear at the bases of the branches and the ends of branches become matted. This must be attended to and all surplus needles picked off as well as those needles which have turned yellow. Unfortunately they have to be removed by hand which is quite a task, considering the sharpness of the needles.

This Juniper should be kept from Winter cold and only exposed to Winter sunshine during the middle of the day. It also needs somewhat special fertilizing, watering and spraying of foliage. Pests are about the same as for other Junipers.

## 10. ARBOR VITAE
### (Konodegashiwa) *Thuja orientalis, Thuja*

The *Thujas* are a group of shrubs or small trees with vertical foliages frequently used as accent plantings in Western landscaping. There are many kinds some of which are too coarse in foliage for dwarfing but others, like the *Thuja orientalis* can be successfully made into miniatures. The foliage of this variety is of a good color and somewhat resembles that of the Hinoki but is not so well regulated in its growth and needs considerable trimming to keep in shape. The trunks of the *Thuja* are fragrant. The Orientals have long considered them an incense tree and they are venerated accordingly.

*Thuja* show to best advantage in Winter when their dense verdure is magnificent. As their case is almost the same as that for the Hinoki, follow the directions for that tree, given later in this chapter, with the additional note that the foliage of the *Thujas* must be carefully gone over and perhaps thinned from time to time to maintain good form.

It would be an interesting experiment to try and dwarf some of the numerous Western *Thujas*. As they are extemely hardy and make masses of easily pruned roots, there should be no great difficulty in producing beautiful dwarfed trees in a comparatively short time.

## 11. ATLANTIC CEDAR
### (Atlas Cedar) *Cedrus atlantica*

The Atlantic Cedar is another tree easily dwarfed. Its short bunched needles, good color and antique form, even in smaller trees, are exceptionally good. Most of the shaping can be done by pruning, and careful wiring. The trees easily accommodate themselves to pot culture. As its name suggests it is a native of the Atlas Mountains of North Africa and one of the three true Cedars.

Propagation is by cuttings usually taken in the Fall and rooted in flats of sand. No special technique is required except that if one wants to speed things, he can use bottom heat and dip the cuttings in a rooting medium. Cuttings do not have to be the same size. Try some large and some small and a surprising number will root.

A. *Three Atlas Cedars about ten years old in a Redwood container.*

B. *A Deodar Cedar, about fifteen years old and two and a half feet tall.*

Atlantic Cedars look well planted in groups. Trees that are not of good form can be combined with their trunks close together so the finished planting has the appearance of a natural clump. Single trees assume good shapes, but generally speaking, the weeping types such as Hanging Cliff Style are not suitable.

The pots used should be low and spreading and of soft colors, or unglazed.

When the new growth has reached an inch or so in length half of it should be removed. Do this either by hand picking or by using sharp shears, taking care to cut the stem only and not the needles. After trimming, new side growth soon appears and in a few years beautiful heads of foliage are established.

Repotting is done every two or three years, in early Spring if the roots are protruding from the drain holes in the bottom of the pot. Remove the tree, shake off about an inch of earth all around and cut those roots which have wound around the inside of the pot. The Atlantic Cedar seems to like fairly good soil so repot in a mixture of five parts sifted garden soil, three parts sand and two parts leaf mold. Be sure to put a layer of coarse material in the bottom of the container. After repotting place in the shade and out of the wind for a couple of weeks. Spray the foliage frequently and at the end of this time bring the plants into the morning sun but never expose them to full sunshine after noon.

Watering is the same as for other dwarf trees, that is, once a day, except in the hottest weather. If the trees are thoroughly hosed with each watering, they should be healthy and free from diseases.

Fertilize with dilute liquid two or three times during the Summer. Chemical or fish fertilizer is good but should be applied with the thought of maintaining the tree's color rather than encouraging new growth, so use in an extremely diluted form.

## 12.   CRYPTOMERIA JAPONICA
### (Sugi)

Visitors to Nikko are surprised at the great size of the Japanese Cryptomerias lining the road and planted throughout the temple areas. Some trees are almost as large as the California Coast Redwoods and, given enough time, eventually attain a diameter of eight or ten feet. One Cryptomeria in a temple garden near Kyoto is over a thousand years old and about the same as a great Sequoia.

There are relatively few good Cryptomeria dwarfed trees. Of the several varieties the usual timber kind is used in making miniatures, though a very small variety, *Cryptomeria globosa,* is sometimes seen but does not have the majesty of the large Cryptomeria.

Trees are propagated from seeds or cuttings or trained from seedlings. Time for transplanting is early Spring. Trees grown from seed or cuttings seldom attain any great distinction. The little trees found under mature specimens are more interesting and another successful method is to make top rootings (layerings) by tying moss over cuts made on branches of good form and keeping the moss wet. Eventually roots grow and the branch makes a good tree. If the bark incision is made in Spring, the roots will show through the moss in Autumn when the branch can be cut off.

Pots for Cryptomerias must have good drainage holes, as usual. For straight trunks use shallows pots with long rectangular shape. If rounded shapes are used the trees will not look as well. Earth colored pots are best.

The Cryptomeria turns a bronzy color in Winter and then, before one realizes, the green of the new season comes out at the ends of the branches. This must be controlled to preserve the shape of the tree. Pinching starts almost at once and is kept up from time to time until Autumn. Do not use shears but pick the new growth off with the fingers. Remove any sprouts from the bottom of the tree. The Cryptomeria has always been thought of as a tree with a straight trunk so when dwarfing, keep this in mind. In the older trees of the forest, lower branches sweep outward and downward, so about April put on wires and train to this style. Cryptomerias bend easily but have tender bark, therefore be careful. When hot weather comes, stop hand picking and wiring.

Repot once every three or four years in late Fall or early Spring. As the Cryptomeria is strong, one can remove practically all of the earth at transplanting time but it is better to leave a good ball whenever possible. Trim the exposed small roots an inch in from the sides of the pot. Potting soil is coarse sandy clay and river sand well mixed in equal amounts. This combination seems to make the roots large and long. While repotting, overly long branches can be trimmed and a compact shape made.

The Cryptomeria likes more moisture than the average. Be sure to maintain a good degree of dampness. Guard against water standing in the bottom of the pot. Fertilizer is given once or twice from the beginning of the new growth to hot weather. September is another month for fertilizing. A dilute liquid is used and if applied a couple of times the Cryptomeria becomes very beautiful.

Cryptomerias want considerable sun but as usual protect from the hot afternoon glare. They are for winter display only. Like the Pines, they have needles and show to best advantage in the Winter.

When cold weather approaches put the Cryptomerias in a frost free location and from time to time take them into the house for viewing. If allowed to become too cold, they turn a red color, diminishing their beauty. After being indoors do not suddenly put them out. Keep under shelter until the worst of Winter is over. When inside be sure the earth is kept moist and every two or three days take them out for watering and washing off of foliage. Do this in the middle of the day when it is as warm as possible. Such treatment helps to discourage insects.

*Wonderful shapes are easily made with the Ezo Spruce as this windswept style at Happo-en, Omiya, Japan, May 1963.*

## 13.  Ezo Spruce

### (Hokkaido Spruce) *Picea jezoensis*

Among dwarfed trees the kinds with large and ancient trunks, twisting shapes and short bunched needles are most popular.  The windswept styles easily developed by the Ezo Spruce naturally fall into this classification.  These beautiful Spruces grow in the high mountains on the main island of Japan and at lower altitudes in the islands to the North, including Hokkaido, Kara-futo and the Kuriles.  They are roughly cone-shaped in form.  There are two varieties of the Ezo Spruce, black and red, the latter being used for dwarfed trees.  It is a relative newcomer to the dwarfed tree family, having first been cultivated around the beginning of this century.  It soon became very popular.  These northern trees are extremely robust, strong in Winter, the branches and needles fine and dense and the trunks having interesting textures.  They have all the appearances of aged trees, and can be trained to Straight Trunks, Groupings, Hanging Cliff Style, Roots Clasping Stones, etc.  All are good.  They are ideal trees for dwarfing with small, dense, deep green needles.

Cuttings are easily made and offer no special difficulties in rooting.  They are taken at two times, in the Spring before the new growth appears and in early Summer after the new growth has hardened.  In both cases be sure to make the cuttings from older vigorous trees.  Cuttings are about one inch long and if taken in early Summer, can be made from the current years' growth.  Flats are prepared by putting some fertile earth in the bottom and covering with sharp sand.  Cuttings are arranged close together in rows.  Flats are then placed in a spot protected from direct sun and wind and frequently sprayed with the hose.  They should be covered with glass or lath to equalize temperature.  Cuttings made in early Spring generally root by the following Autumn.  Those made in early Summer should root by the following Spring.  Cuttings made in Summer seem to root a little better.

The colors of the pots should harmonize with the tree.  Containers approaching earth color are generally seen.  Occasionally, in order to accentuate a tree, an off white is used.  If the trees have straight trunks, one uses flat rectangular pots or flat elliptical pots.  For the styles such as cliff, etc., where branches are trained to hang over the pots, one uses pots of a round or square design.

The Ezo Spruce must be repotted about every three years.  This is generally done around the Spring equinox or earlier.  Repotting is also successful in Autumn.

*Ezo Spruce. (Opposite page)*
*A.  Wonderful shapes are easily made with this variety.*
*B.  Double-trunked Ezo Spruce, with down-sweeping branches.*
*C.  Older specimens are amazingly beautiful.*

Potting soil is coarse, sandy clay, four parts, and sand three parts, well mixed. For older trees a soil composed of four parts screened garden earth, four parts sand and two parts of leaf mold is desirable. In removing trees from their pots, try to leave smaller roots and trim off the larger. Leave long new roots and cut off the older. It is important to handle the roots carefully.

Wiring is done from the last of October through March. One should take the time necessary to compose good shapes. Minor adjustments of contour, using very thin wire can be made any time in the year. Do the main wiring in the Winter and in May or June correct the branch ends.

These trees like full morning sun with shade from twelve o'clock on. Afternoon sun damages the color of the needles.

Water in heat and in cold. As it is a conifer and as its treatment is the same as for a Pine, it needs lots of water. However in the coldest weather do not give so much water that the earth in the pot will freeze.

Fertilizer is applied from Spring to Summer. After the Autumn equinox fertilizing is again resumed. A dilute liquid is used very sparingly, more to keep the trees in condition than to cause new growth.

Diseases are about the same as for Pine trees. The best remedy is sprinkling of foliage and keeping the soil moist.

Bunched needles sometimes need attention. Thin them by hand picking about April. The bunches should be thinned from the tips toward the trunk. At the same time do general shaping.

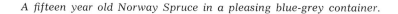

*A fifteen year old Norway Spruce in a pleasing blue-grey container.*

## 14.  NOTES ON WESTERN SPRUCES

Many American and European Spruces are excellent for dwarfing.  Among them may be mentioned *Picea Excelsa,* the Norway Spruce and *Picea Pungens,* the Colorado Blue Spruce.  The Norway Spruce is ideal, especially in its more compact varieties.  All the directions for the care of the Ezo-Spruce apply to the Norway kinds with the addition that trimmings from the Norway Spruce, if fully matured, can be rooted at almost any time.  This makes it easy to root parts removed in pruning.  These soon produce nice little trees on their own.  When wiring the Norway Spruce be careful in bending larger branches as they sometimes split at the crotch.  Styles most suited to the Norway Spruce are Multiple Trunk, Single Trees, and Roots Grasping Stones.  In thinning these trees try to prune more or less in layers by cutting off the twigs and branches that reach up and down.  When properly thinned and trained, Spruces are among the most attractive of the needle-bearing dwarfed trees.

Spruce varieties can with a little care be made into compact and interesting trees.  Other forms of the Norway Spruce easy to dwarf are: *Picea Excelsa Mucronata*—Dwarf Norway Spruce, *Picea Excelsa Nudiformis*—Nest Spruce, and *Picea Excelsa Pygmaea*—Pygmy Spruce.

The Colorado Blue Spruce should have its new growth trimmed back two thirds each year to give the necessary tight form.  Its color, however, is so beautiful that this added work is justified.

*Reverse side of Norway Spruce shown on opposite page.*

*Various Chamaecyparis*

   A. *An older specimen of the Sawara Cypress.*

   B. *Two smaller Sawaras.*

   C. *Dwarfed Lawson Cypresses.*

## 15.  HINOKI CYPRESS

(Japanese Cypress) *Chamaecyparis obtusa*

To many Occidentals these little trees represent the very essence of the Orient. Some consider them the most beautiful of all and larger ones are cherished as specimens in many gardens. Because of the compact and horizontal design of their fan-like branches, they are about perfect for pot culture. There is a swirling design to the foliage not found in any other conifer and this, together with the interesting bark pattern, creates a beautiful effect.

The Hinoki occurs in quite a number of varieties, from the one used for timber—a slow growing, rather sparse tree that makes magnificent lumber, to the garden kinds. The latter are by nature dwarfed to varying degrees. Some have green foliage, others golden, and the smallest grows only a few inches a year but has layer upon layer of ruffled verdure, puffed out like a quail's feathers on a cold morning. These last are the most useful for dwarfing and for training to artistic shapes.

The name 'Hinoki' means 'Fire Tree.' The ancients worshiped it as a source of fire, as, growing in dense forests, high wind occasionally rubbed trunks together causing conflagrations. When made into dwarfed trees the Hinokis are vigorous like Chinese Junipers but less solemn in appearance; have extremely neat shapes and, while not twisting into exotic curves, are harmonious and a pleasure to behold. This is especially so when one of a group is planted on stones and arranged to represent a section of a forest.

The culture of the Hinoki is not as simple as that of the Junipers. The difficult point is the forming of the proper tree shapes, mostly by pruning. All dwarfed tree growers seem to have this difficulty—a poor method of pruning quickly ruins the tree. The procedure most generally favored is as follows: first trim the ends of the little branches as if one were making round leaves, then, studying one of these 'leaves,' trim it roughly to heart shape, that is, with a broader outer end, slightly indented in the center. The point of the heart is toward the trunk of the tree. Do the job slowly and carefully, considering each branch as it comes in turn. If pruning is neglected the branches have a tendency to elongate and begin to shed many of the needles nearest the trunk creating bare spots and a general air of disorder. If one wants a short cut, the pinching back of new growth will keep the tree in fairly good shape but the individual branches will not have the elegance seen in better cared-for specimens. Shapes—Straight Trunks and Hanging Cliff Styles are good. Hinokis have lots of branches and the trees are thinned in Winter so that the young growth will not be too dense. The Hinokis keep on growing from Spring to Autumn so one must constantly pick off surplus foliage. If one uses shears to do this, the cut places change color and the tree loses its beauty.

The beginning of Spring is an excellent time for repotting the Hinoki.

The very best season is when the average temperature has risen to around sixty degrees.  One should not miss this time as there is no other as satisfactory.  The Hinoki is temperamental and if repotted at an unfavorable time, becomes weakened and for a whole year refuses to grow.  Spring is also the one time for putting small wires on the ends of branches, but once wired they must not be touched for a whole year.  There are those who worry about this, saying if they leave the wires for the year, the branches may develop wounds but this is the lesser evil as the bark is soft like that on some Maples and, although wounds may be made, they heal rapidly.

Fertilizers used are on the weak nitrogenous side and only occasionally resorted to.  Most liquid fertilizers would be suitable.

The Hinoki is kept in the same location as any other dwarfed tree—that is, one with a good circulation of air, but not unduly exposed to wind and the same general prohibition holds about subjecting them to the late afternoon sun.  If allowed to dry out, the ends of the twigs die and turn an ugly brown.  So place them in a location having morning sun and afternoon shade and water at least once a day.  Those planted in wooden containers are less likely to dry than those in pottery or porcelain pots so the latter should be watered more frequently.

Cuttings can be made from the Hinoki in the usual way but are slow in rooting and growing.  It is best to use bottom heat.  But if one is willing to embark on a lengthy project covering a good many years, the growing of Hinoki from cuttings is eventually rewarding.

The following varieties of *Chamaecyparis* make good dwarfed trees:

*Chamaecyparis obtusa*—Hinoki Cypress
*Chamaecyparis obtusa compacta*—Compact Hinoki Cypress
*Chamaecyparis obtusa compacta nana*—Dwarfed Hinoki Cypress
*Chamaecyparis pisifera filifera*—Thread Cypress
*Chamaecyparis lawsoniana ellwoodi*—Ellwood Cypress
*Chamaecyparis lawsoniana spinosa viralis*—Dwarf Blue Lawson Cypress
*Chamaecyparis pisifera squarrosa*—Silver Cypress
*Chamaecyparis pisifera plumosa*—Plume Cypress
*Chamaecyparis wisseli*—Wissel Cypress
*Chamaecyparis pisifera aurea compacta nana*—Sawara Cypress

## 16.  CALIFORNIA COAST REDWOOD
### (Bei Sugi) *Sequoia sempervirens*

Almost everyone interested in dwarfed trees has thought of trying his luck with Redwoods but how to make miniatures of such huge affairs has generally been a puzzling question.  While Redwoods do present some difficulties and take more time than most, they can be successfully dwarfed.  One of the really unusual points about them is their habit of forming trunks with miniature burls, suggesting in their shapes the full grown trees.

The propagation of the Redwoods is either by seeds or cuttings or small seedlings dug in the forest. As the Redwood is a member of the acid-loving Cryptomeria group, the seeds are gathered in the Fall, mixed with peat moss and well decayed leaf mold and put in a container with poor drainage. The mixture should be mounded so that the bottom will be in a saturated condition and the top slightly less wet. Place in the shade and renew the water constantly. By spring the young Redwoods will be seen growing in considerable numbers. From then on they are potted up in the same mixture in which they were started with the addition of some sifted sandy clay.

All Redwood trees are not alike. Some have branches which reach upward while other varieties weep in the manner of Willows. When making cuttings, select a suitable tree and with a sharp knife make as many cuttings as needed, limiting their length to three or four inches. Take a nurseryman's flat and put about an inch of peat moss in the bottom and fill the rest with coarse river sand. Dip the ends of the cuttings in some rooting material, place them close together in the flat and put the flat in a warm shady location. Keep well moistened. The cuttings will root in about half a year.

Redwoods should be trained to Straight Trunks as this is their natural form. They may be grown singly or in the circular groups so frequently seen in Redwood forests. When a mature Redwood is cut, a circle of sprouts quickly grows around the stump, developing into a ring of second growth trees. This same design should be followed in the grouping of miniature Redwoods.

Trimming is rather difficult. The new growth of young Redwoods consists of needles more than branches. These needles are nicely arranged in a symmetrical manner. The trick is to pinch off all new growth to half an inch in length. New buds form on the pinched off ends making two sprouts where before there was but one. The pinching must be constant. After a few years the trunks begin to take on good form and eventually the branches shape up.

Repotting is not too vital a matter. The Redwood is more interested in moisture than potting earth. A spongy medium composed of peat moss, leaf mold and sandy clay is ideal. After several years when the pots have become filled with roots, the outer inch or so of soil and roots can be trimmed off and the trees repotted. Late Fall or early Spring are both good times for this. Pots used for Redwoods are of the broad, shallow variety.

Wiring is a necessity in training the limbs. Redwoods are easily bent so there is no difficulty in this. An easy way is to make simple 'S' shapes of wire, securing the lowest to the pot by means of string and using the rest, one above the other, in pulling down the layers of branches. Redwoods do best in a shady location with some morning sun. Keep wet at all times. If a dilute liquid fertilizer is given once or twice in the Summer it is helpful in maintaining a good color. Any fish or commercial fertilizer would do. If the above directions are followed, Redwoods should not have diseases. As their name *"Sempervirens"* signifies, they are not easily discouraged.

# CHAPTER 5.

## *Broad-Leaved and Deciduous Trees*

### INTRODUCTION

The number of broad-leaved and deciduous trees that can be successfully dwarfed is many times that of the Needle-Bearing kinds, and the results, while perhaps not as solemn in feeling, are extremely varied and enjoyable. The broad-leaved and deciduous trees almost always have flowers, or colorful foliages, or interesting patterns not found in the Pines or similar varieties; the losing of leaves, the naked branches of Winter, the buddings of Spring, and the glorious colors of Autumn make Maples the delight of all Dwarfed Tree fanciers, while the glossy leaves of Camellias with their exquisite blooms, sometimes opening while still snowbound, offer an extremely poetic touch. Plums, of course, are the main standby in the deciduous field. Blooming, like the Camellias, in the cold of late Winter, they are the subjects of innumerable poems and legends. Other similar trees and plants lending themselves to pot culture include the Pomegranate, Wisterias, Azaleas, Crepe Myrtles, and Flowering Quinces, to mention only a few spectacular examples. Bamboos and Willows grown for their cool green foliages, to be appreciated in Summer, are equally fascinating. The enthusiast will quickly add many local trees and plants to this classification, and try his luck at dwarfing seedlings of Holly, Acacia, Broom, Manzanita, Bay, Oak, Blueberry, Cotoneaster and so on—whatever is available. Almost anything can at least be tried, and the successes greatly outnumber failures.

*Azaleas make spectacular bonsai and can be planted in colorful pots.*

# 1. AZALEAS

## (Tsutsuji) *Rhododendron indicum*

About twenty years ago Azaleas were still a comparative rarity in Western gardens. Generally priced above other shrubs they were sparingly planted in smaller homes. But today due to greatly improved methods of propagation Azaleas are no longer expensive and are available in any number of varieties, colors and growing habits. The Japanese take delight in dwarfing the *Indicum* types.

These are the small leafed Azaleas, mostly evergreen that occur in a number of varieties, foliages and colors. Many are used for general landscaping. The flowers open at definite times so there are early to late bloomings. When the buds unfurl plants are brought indoors out of the weather and too bright sunshine. This allows a longer time for their appreciation. Every three or four days the plants are taken outside and placed in the weak morning sunshine for two or three hours. When the flowers have finished, dead blossoms are removed by hand picking.

Propagation is done by cuttings taken from the hardened new growth. These are placed in sharp sand and kept well watered, and in a month or two start making roots. Azaleas are generally shown in deep pots as their shapes spread and cascade in a horizontal design. Famous old trees have thick trunks. The contrast of the masses of delicate blossoms against the ancient bark is always pleasing. After the plants have finished blooming they are trimmed. All unwanted branches are removed, and, as the effect of the large trunk needs to be emphasized, ends of remaining branches are shortened. Also any growth not absolutely essential to the shape of the tree is eliminated. If this is done before late Spring new sprouts may come out near the cut places, but these can be cut off as necessary. But if Spring growth is trimmed back too early there is a chance of injuring the next blooming, so only the long growth is entirely removed. In the following May the remaining slightly trimmed branches will bloom normally.

When the flowers have finished, repot with new earth. Azaleas should be repotted each year and the larger roots slightly trimmed. Repotting soil should avoid the clay side. Black loam five parts, sand five parts and leaf mold three parts make a good mixture. As the Azaleas are plants that grow in masses under the shade of evergreens they should be placed in shade after 2 p.m. In the heat of Summer it is best to protect them with a lath covering. One must be sure to have a good circulation of air at all times to prevent the development of pests.

In ordinary weather watering is done once a day. If protected by lath, even in Summer once a day should suffice. If no protection is available give enough water to keep from drying. It is an excellent idea to thoroughly spray the foliage morning and evening, using the garden hose and one's finger instead of a nozzle. In Winter water once in two or three days.

Dilute liquid fertilizer can be given in early Spring after blooming and in late Summer.

Wiring is done in the middle of May. As Azaleas are rather brittle they cannot stand much bending.

Sometimes the centers of the buds are chewed by small insects which can be eliminated by a nicotine spray used every ten days.

## 2.  BAMBOOS

(Kanchiku)   *Arundinaria marmorea*
(Mosochiku)  *Phyllostachys edulis*
(Hoteichiku) *Phyllostachys reticulata*

The Bamboos are a fascinating group. Consisting of several hundreds of varieties of all sizes, colors, shapes (there is even a square bamboo—*Arundinaria quadrangularis*), the array is most confusing. In size they range from the dwarf kinds only a few inches tall to the Indian varieties with a diameter of over a foot. This latter grows to a height of sixty or more feet at the unbelievable rate of eighteen inches or more a day! In colors there are, in addition to the green stemmed and foliaged kinds, those of golden shades, or golden foliage with pure black stems, or golden stems spotted black. Then there are the striped kinds— leaves edged with silver or gold, and stem striped with brilliant green on yellow. Altogether these plants are amazing.

The three varieties mentioned at the top of this section are the usual ones from which miniatures are made, and the way of doing it, in keeping with the general spirit of bamboos, is again unusual.

In Japan from the end of April to the middle of May, sections of Bamboo roots about six inches long are dug and planted in shallow pottery containers. A layer of leaf mold and rotted straw is placed in the bottoms of the

*Bamboo is fun to try but takes considerable work.*

pots. On this the roots are laid and covered with a mixture of leaf mold and sandy clay. The trays are then placed in a sunny location, kept well watered, and left undisturbed until the following Spring. The sprouts begin growing about a month after potting and continue to grow until Winter with its cold stops them.

When Spring arrives, all mixed and crossed foliage is thinned, and all stems that are not straight cut off. When the new Spring sprouts have grown to a height of five or six inches, uncover their bases and carefully peel off the bottom sheath next to the root. This sheath is very much alive, and by removing it, sprouts are either stopped entirely or greatly slowed in their growth. In this way the Bamboo can be regulated to the height desired.

Bamboo is a vigorous grower and is repotted each Spring. Potting soil is a mixture of leaf mold and black loam in about equal amounts with about a quarter of sand added. After repotting give sufficient water and for a month or two apply dilute liquid fertilizer (fish emulsion, etc.) every other week. Don't fertilize in the heat of Summer or in Winter.

If the first crop of leaves is trimmed off about the end of June, the new foliage will be in top shape for Summer and Autumn.

Aphids and Woolly Aphids like Bamboo. Be sure to wash the under sides of the leaves, the stems, and especially the places where the leaves and twigs branch from larger stalks. A vigorous washing with the hose in the evening should keep them healthy.

Bamboos like a considerable amount of sun but should be shaded in the hottest weather. They don't stand cold very well, so must be protected in Winter.

### 3. CAMELLIA

#### (Tsubaki) *Camellia japonica*

Camellias are considered rustic members of the dwarfed tree family. The luster of the new leaves contrasting with the brown of stems and flower sheaths, the flame colored flowers with their golden masses of stamens and the ornamental nature of the branch growth, make Camellias the glory of early Spring. They vie with the Plums and Flowering Quinces and it can truly be said that the Camellia well represents the two elements "Spring and tree" which compose its written form in Chinese.

The Camellia lacks the fragrance of the Plum, neither has it the gorgeousness of certain Cherries, and although the variety most often seen is of the deepest red color, there is no forced or oversophisticated feeling. It blooms in a natural manner and falls naturally; it awakens within us an appreciation of its quiet loveliness.

A famous Japanese poet Morikawa Kyoroku says in his "Chronicle of a Hundred Flowers," "The Camellia, like a good wife, does not imitate the too colorful attire of certain persons but attends to her duties within the home. She keeps her emotions under control and in waiting upon others displays her femininity. She uses no makeup and conducts herself like a flower." However in Japan there is a strange superstition among some people that the Camellia is unlucky. The reason is that the Camellia blossom suddenly drops in one piece like a young warrior losing his head in combat.

Among the Camellias there are varieties that make large seed pods, peony flowered kinds, double varieties, long flowering kinds that bloom for several months, red, white and variegated varieties and many others. But those used for dwarfing are almost always the wild variety that grows naturally in the fields. This is called in Japanese the Yamatsubaki (Mountain Camellia). There is also the Kantsubaki (Cold Camellia) that opens its flowers in late Winter. The cold-flowering kind blooms the last of March and the Spring Flowering variety blooms in April and May.

The Camellia is propagated by seeds or cuttings. The better plants being grown from the former, but as seedlings take some time to develop and do not come true to type, cuttings are generally used. Grafting is only occasionally resorted to. Cuttings are made from this years' matured wood taken in Summer about the latter part of July. As they take some time to root it is best to treat them with a rooting compound and put them in a frame with bottom heat.

The potting soil for Camellias should be on the acid side. They prefer a rich, light well-drained acid loam. The combination used for dwarfing is seven parts of sifted loam mixed with three parts of coarse sandy clay. Put sifted earth, the finer particles discarded, and sand in the bottoms of the pots for good drainage. When planting, firm the earth around the roots, using a stick. Cut any roots that tend to go around the edges of the pot and don't poke the earth too hard so as to make a solid mass and prevent roots from spreading. Repot about the latter part of March.

Wiring is applied while the new growth is yet pliable and sprouts are not too long. Otherwise there is danger of injuring them. As the bark is tender in Spring it is best to wrap the wire in paper before putting it on. If the wires are applied too tightly they will cut into the soft bark. It is necessary to loosen the wires toward the end of September.

Camellias are placed in a location having a considerable amount of sunshine and a good circulation of air, but being by nature shade loving shrubs are protected in Summer by lath or by being moved to a shady location. When Autumn comes and the plants have been exposed to one or two frosts, they are moved to a protected place.

Some varieties will bloom if taken into a cold frame or Winter storehouse and given a slight amount of heat. While blooming they are protected from cold and wind and when the flowers are finished, slightly trimmed so that seeds will not set.

Camellias like a considerable amount of water so are sprinkled frequently.

In Spring the Camellias develop their new growth and begin to set buds, and a certain amount of a care is necessary to see they have enough fertilizer. During the heat of Summer they are given dilute fertilizer every couple of weeks. This is stopped about the end September. It is a good rule to water after each fertilizing as too strong an application might hurt the roots.

Scale and aphids sometimes damage the plants and one must be on the watch against these.

## CAMELLIA SAZANKWA

The Sazankwas are now being recognized as extremely useful and beautiful members of the Camellia family. Their single flowers of delicate coloring, while not as spectacular as those of the better known Camellia varieties, harmonize perfectly with the spirit of dwarfed trees. In earliest Spring when blossoms are rare and snow still lingers, the Sazankwas are indeed welcome. Some even bloom in Winter and the sight of their apparently delicate blossoms opening in snow-powdered foliage is a most cheering one. Colors range from pure white to white splashed and tinged with scarlet. The usual kinds have only a blush of color at the ends of the petals and this framing of the central mass of golden stamens is all the more pronounced because of the general dullness of the chilly season.

The Sazankwas make a fairly heavy root growth and are usually repotted each year about the time of the Spring equinox. The potting soil is coarse sifted sandy clay, three parts and black loam four parts. The Sazankwas produce flowers on the ends of the current years' growth and have the habit of making altogether too long shoots, so there is always the question of sacrificing one or the other. A compromise has been worked out as follows: Cut back this years' growth to suit the shape of the tree and leave the new growth on the already trimmed wood of the previous year. This allows the enjoying of bloom and at the same time adequately controls the shape of the tree.

Wiring is applied in May or June but only on the new growth. If done in a careless manner it will cut into the bark, making unsightly bumps and also interfere with the formation of flowers.

Unlike most Camellias the Sazankwas like the sun but of course must be kept well watered. So in order to make good roots place in a sunny spot except in hot weather.

Propagation is from seeds unless special characteristics of parent plants are desired, when they can be grafted or started from cuttings. However the seedlings are generally satisfactory and have a variety of bloom more suited to the dwarfed tree grower's taste.

Fertilizing is done fairly soon after repotting to encourage new root growth. It is applied in a dilute liquid form two or three times in the

Spring, with a slightly heavier application just after the flowers have finished. An acid fertilizer suitable for Azaleas is best.

As the Sazankwas do not mind the cold there is no need to protect them in Winter. However in the severest weather it wouldn't hurt to move them into a somewhat sheltered location, more to protect the pots from freezing than injury to the plants. If the Sazankwas are allowed to bloom year after year they are eventually weakened and lose much of their charm so it is well to give them one year of rest in ever three or four, picking off any buds that form.

## 4. CHERRIES

### (Sakura)

*Prunus serrulate spontanea—Prunus subhirtella pendula—Prunus yedoensis*

It is difficult to think of Japan without visualizing Cherry blossoms. The Single Cherry is the National flower of the Japanese and to their mind most fully expresses the Japanese spirit. Their books are illustrated with scenes of young warriors practicing archery under Cherry trees, Mount Fuji seen through branches of Cherry blossoms, or an ancient castle with its white walls reflecting the pink of the Cherries. No wonder the Japanese go to great lengths in making dwarfed trees of suitable varieties. The Cherries used in landscaping are innumerable but those dwarfed are mainly from one strain, the Mountain Cherry (Yama Zakura) or *Prunus serrulata*. Other varieties of Cherry have excellent flowers but do not always have the form for dwarfing. The Mountain Cherry is native to the Northeastern part of Japan. The tree form is elegant, flowers and leaves open at the same time, and buds and flowers are tinged with crimson. The contrast with the foliage is beautiful. From this strain of Cherries several widely used kinds for dwarfing have been developed.

First is the Mount Fuji Cherry (Fuji Zakura). This is very popular. Compared with the Mountain Cherry, the flowers are smaller and the ends of the petals are deeply indented. The color of the buds is light crimson with the opening flowers turning to white. There is a smaller form of the Mount Fuji Cherry which is called the Miniature Cherry (Mame Zakura). Still another variety has somewhat greenish blossoms. Also there are single kinds, double kinds and varieties that cascade. All the leaves resemble those of the Mountain Cherry, being rather slender and having saw-toothed edges. In some varieties the leaves sprout after the flowers have finished. The bark has a reddish tinge and a weathered appearance of age. As it is a native of near Alpine regions the trunks are rather small and the branches complicated. In making them into dwarfed trees these natural tendencies are kept in mind. Their cultivation is rather difficult and it takes a good deal of doing to keep them blooming year after year.

There is another Cherry called the Cold Season Cherry (Kan Zakura).

*Seventy-year-old Mountain Cherry at Kyuka-en Bonsai Gardens, near Omiya, Japan, showing blossoms on March 20, 1960 (above). Repotted in April, lower photo shows foliage on September 20, 1960. (Top photo courtesy of Mr. Kyuzo Murata of Kyuka-en.)*

It blooms earlier, which accounts for the name. It is descended from the wild Cherry that grows in the upper parts of the high mountains in Formosa. Flowers are pale scarlet, and the leaves and flowers develop about the same time. One variety is called the Spring Equinox Cherry (Higan Zakura) and has the deepest scarlet coloring, with a drooping habit of branching and doesn't grow very tall, but is an excellent variety for dwarfing. A variation of the Spring Equinox Cherry is called the October Cherry (Ju Gatsu Zakura) and blooms both in the Spring and in the Autumn and is a rare kind.

Cherries have the unfortunate habit of whole branches suddenly dying. The mountain Cherry strain is not quite so subject to this defect. Cherries also make too many roots and stronger trees will completely fill their pots by the beginning of Summer. It is imperative that they be repotted each year. This may be safely done from the time of leaf falling to the following April or before new growth appears. When repotting leave thirty or forty percent of the old earth, cut off the roots that circle around the pot and any others that protrude from the remaining earth. If repotting takes place after the flowering period of the Winter blooming kinds, about half of the original earth should be left.

Potting soil is a mixture of the coarser parts of sandy clay earth, black peat soil and river sand. In ancient times the potting soils for Cherries were based on a considerable percentage of sand but present day ideas call for more earth.

Pots used are of near earth colors, of forms suited to the individual tree. As the Cherry is a sun loving tree it is perfectly safe to place it in a sunny location immediately following repotting but guard against strong winds for a couple of weeks. After that, until the first of June place in full sun and in a good current of air. This will strengthen the new twigs. Before June the form of the tree and the tendency to bloom the following year can be improved by shaping the new foliage. From June on protect it from the western sun so the leaves will not burn.

Wiring can be done about the middle of April just after flowering. At the same time clip off unwanted branches and trim the new sprouts. If this trimming is done too early it will injure the next year's blooming, so do not start while there are still flowers on the tree.

The leaves of the Cherry are large and absorb considerable moisture. For this reason Cherries must be kept moist at all times.

In fertilizing avoid using material of an animal origin. Dilute commercial fertilizers applied after blooming will help. As the Cherry takes a lot of special watering in Summer, fertilizing is completely stopped at that time as it tends to start root decay. Trees are fertilized once more in Autumn.

Cherries have many pests. Caterpillars, scale, aphids, wire worms, etc.— all like the Cherry. One must constantly be on guard and ready to repulse offending insects.

## 5. CREPE MYRTLE

(Hyaku-Jitsu-ko—100 Days of Scarlet)
(Saru-Suberi—Tree-too-Smooth-For-Monkeys-To-Climb)
*Lagerstroemia indica*

The Crepe Myrtle is another of those spectacular small trees with handsome racemes of flowers and extremely smooth and colorful bark. It grows to a height of about twenty feet and is known among the Japanese as the 'hundred day flowering.' The original variety is scarlet. There are lavender, lavender scarlets, scarlet and white mixtures, and pure whites. There is also a rare variety that is light yellow, but usually the scarlet kinds are seen. Making this beautiful tree conform to the limited life of a potted plant is rather difficult.

The Crepe Myrtle is propagated by seeds sown in Spring or cuttings of ripe wood taken in the Fall. As usual in preparing the cuttings, some rooting medium should be used and if possible bottom heat applied.

The Crepe Myrtle naturally twists and turns so the making of tree shapes can usually be done by proper pruning. Specimen single trees are generally grown and are planted in pots of lighter glazes than the average. This is especially true at the time of flowering when interesting combinations can be thought out, depending upon the color of the flowers.

The Crepe Myrtle must have plenty of heat. For this reason one endeavors to make it bloom in the hottest part of Summer. About the beginning of Summer the new growth is pinched back and the second new growth will have flowers without too greatly damaging the shape of the tree. Most of the flowers are borne on the current year's wood and as the Crepe Myrtle has the unfortunate habit of sending out Spring shoots at a great rate there is always the problem of having flowers and yet not losing the shape of the tree. In order to make it bloom in Mid-Summer considerable fertilizing is necessary.

Potting is done every year without fail, in early Spring. Break off one half or more of the old earth, trim the small roots and put plenty of gravel in the bottom of the pot, to assure good drainage.

Potting soil is three parts sandy clay, six parts black loam and one or two parts of leaf mold. At the time of repotting the entire shape of the tree can be gone over even to the trimming off of unwanted last year's growth, but from every trimmed branch two or three new sprouts will shoot out and these must be thinned. After repotting do not fertilize for about a month. But from then until the time of blooming give dilute liquid fertilizer (fish or chemical) once each week. It is a good idea to give an application of bone meal every two or three weeks. Give plenty of water.

As the Crepe Myrtle likes heat, put it in full sun. It grows rapidly and the sun soon dries it out so some days it must be watered several times. About the beginning of Summer correct the shape of the tree, cutting a little

Crepe Myrtle loves heat and does not do well in the North.

A. Crepe Myrtle in Summer—notice the white pot.

B. Ancient trunk of an old specimen, best displayed in Winter.

short. If one is careful in watering, new sprouts will immediately start. Sometimes trimming will have to be done twice. Trimming alone will not always preserve the shape of the tree so from May to July one can put on wires if necessary. Wires are put on two year old branches and if done properly the shape of the tree will be corrected by Autumn.

The Crepe Myrtle cannot stand cold and must be protected in Winter. At the beginning of Summer aphids attack the new buds. Daily washing of foliage with a spray of water is usually sufficient to control them.

## 6. FLOWERING CRABAPPLE

### (Kaido) *Malus Floribunda*

Of all the Spring Blossoms, those of the different apples hold a special place in our affections and memories. Because they are among the last to bloom and have a charm of their own, they are more nostalgic than most. Who has not seen an abandoned apple orchard with two or three ancient and broken trees still putting forth sweetly scented blossoms? And among the Apple varieties none are more charming than the Flowering Crabs.

These smaller Apples make spectacular dwarfed trees. The Japanese have two varieties for this type of work. One is called the Hanakaido (Flowering Crabapple) and the other is Miyama Kaido (the Crab from Miyama). The flowers of the Hanakaido variety are the more beautiful and one variation is the hanging thread type where the flower stems are extra long and hang downward when in bloom. Another kind has short stems and the flowers are held erect. This is called the Ukezaki Kaido (the Crab from Ukezaki). The flowers of both kinds have numbers of buds of a blending of crimson and lavender, turning to a fainter crimson when open. The shapes of the Flowering Crabs are not too good but as the plants cover themselves with bloom they are cultivated as flowering dwarfed trees.

The Miyama Kaido has a fairly deep crimson color with a lighter crimson lining. The foliage is light green and comes out at the same time as the flowers. In Autumn red fruits are born on the ends of the twigs, and considering it under the classification of fruiting shrubs, it is magnificent.

Propagation is chiefly done by grafting on to seedling root stock, much the same as one would do with any named variety of Apple.

The trees are planted in fairly deep containers as they usually have shapes that tend to cascade. They are seldom planted in groups but are usually cultivated as specimen trees.

It is necessary to repot each year in early Spring while still dormant. Discard about two thirds of the earth, trim any roots that are superfluous and put coarse sandy clay in the bottom of the pot over a layer of gravel as it especially likes water. Repotting soil is an equal mixture of sandy clay and loam. In potting a young tree and wishing to retard the growth, put it in as small a pot as possible.  If one wants to develop smaller leaves and fruits, after the flowers have finished at the beginning of Summer, pick off any of the remaining parts of the blossoms, and cut off about two thirds of the new growth.  After this main pruning new sprouts immediately grow and of these two or three twigs on each branch are left and the rest cut off.  In early Spring always keep the wild new growth cut back.  The Flowering Crab will bloom from the larger branches and even the trunk, so it is important that new growth be pinched back to preserve the shape of the tree.

If wiring must be done, Spring is best.  There is considerable danger of breaking limbs or of separating the bark from the heartwood so be careful.  Wires are loosened in Autumn.

As the Kaido will not stand cold it is brought into the house about the time of the first frost.  Aphids sometimes attack the leaves but don't do much damage.

## 7.  FLOWERING QUINCE

### (Boke) *Chaenomeles lagenaria*

In recent years the Flowering Quince has undergone great improvement in color and size of blossoms.  Most Western gardens have two or three of these popular plants, useful for flower arrangements as well as outdoor beauty.  Colors now range from deep red to pure white, with all possible intermediate combinations.  The Flowering Quinces have much to be said in their favor.  Beside their two main flowerings in Spring they bear scattered blossoms over a period of at least half the year.  The present varieties have great vigor and from the point of dwarfing are exceptionally good as their gnarled trunks and interesting fruits in the Autumn fit in nicely with both Spring and Autumn classifications.

The propagation of Flowering Quinces is simple.  Some of the best dwarfed trees are made by digging plants from the garden and adapting them to pots, but the usual method is by cutting or layering.  Cuttings are made in the Fall in the usual manner and should have roots by the following Spring.  After this they are potted up but it takes several years before they amount to anything.

The trees can be trained into fantastic shapes.  The natural irregularities of the branches are artistic and can easily be encouraged to grow into the more or less cascading forms.  Pots are either shallow or fairly deep, according to the type of plant and are more colorful than usual.  Deep red Flowering Quinces look well in greyed-lavender pots, but the pure white pots are not too interesting.  It would be better to keep to the soft greens or terra-cotta colors.

Repotting is done in the middle of October before the weather becomes cold. This allows the plant to establish itself and have time to set buds for Spring flowering. Potting soil is sandy clay two parts, leaf mold two parts and sand one part, all well mixed. Specimens with large trunks dug from the field or bought from the nursery do not object to rather severe root pruning. Cutting the larger roots is safe, but all hair roots possible should be preserved. After repotting place in a sunny location and water sufficiently. Be sure to keep damp or damage results. In Summer especially the Flowering Quinces must not be allowed to dry. Evening sprinkling of the foliage is a good idea.

When the flowers are finished, pick off all remaining dried petals and give the plants a general going-over. This is a good time to fertilize. Some commercial fertilizer and bone meal mixed make a fine combination. Sprinkle this in the pot in two or three places and water well. Also apply dilute liquid fertilizer once or twice in late Summer, to assure good growth and blooming but if it forces too long branches be sure to cut these back to two or three leaves. At the time of Autumn repotting, the trees can have their final trimming.

After December place the Flowering Quinces in a sunny but protected location to preserve them from damage by cold.

These plants are subject to attacks by aphids, and should have their foliage frequently washed with the hose.

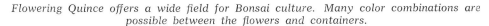

*Flowering Quince offers a wide field for Bonsai culture. Many color combinations are possible between the flowers and containers.*

## 8.  FORSYTHIA

### (Rengyo) *Forsythia suspensa*

The West knows the Forsythia as a spreading half-climbing shrub with slender arching branches, but the Japanese make very good dwarfed trees from this unlikely material.  As it blooms well, the flowers opening about the end of March before the plant has put out leaves, the effect is extremely fresh and colorful and accents the spirit of the season.  The flowers are bold and set opposite each other and from one spot two or three blossoms will open at the same time, making a truly beautiful display.

Propagation is easily done with cuttings or by layering.  The cuttings develop into very good dwarfed trees.  An interesting variation in the usual tree formation is made by planting two or three rooted cuttings tightly together and twisting them so as to eventually form a beautiful trunk.  The ends of the cuttings can be trained into the main branches of the tree.

The shapes most appropriate to Forsythia are Straight Trunks, Connected Trunks and Cliff Hanging.  All are rather interesting.  As the branches are so long and sweeping the building up of good shapes is difficult but by continual pruning and wiring a satisfactory plant will eventually result.  It is easy for the plant to grow out of shape.

Repot each year after blooming using soil composed of half garden earth and sand.  It likes a considerable amount of sun and there is not much need for fertilizer.  However occasional applications of liquid manure up to July might help.

## 9.  GINKO

### (Ichyo) *Ginko biloba*—Maidenhair tree

The Ginko is one of the unique trees of the world.  In geological times it grew over much of the Northern Hemisphere and fossil remains are found in such widely separated places as Asia and North America.  It is the only survival in its genus.  Fortunately for us this most unusual tree is now available in most nurseries and has again been widely distributed.  The Orientals consider it the most beautiful of the Autumn yellow leafed trees.  Originally found in China, it was brought to Japan at some date lost to history.  The trees are male and female.  The female has nuts which are unusual for a dwarfed tree.  The leaves closely resemble those of the Maidenhair fern and the older the tree the more beautifully indented they become.  In Spring and Summer the Ginko is a soft green but in Autumn the large trees turn into tall golden pillars that can be seen for miles.

Propagation is by seed, cuttings and grafting.  The usual method is from seed unless special characteristics are to be transmitted.  An easy way for doing this is to make a seed bed in some protected corner of the garden, sow

A. Twin Ginko trees in Summer.
B. A single large trunk in Winter, showing the upward thrusting branches.

A

B

the seeds and then transfer the young seedlings to pots. When grown from seeds the branches, leaves, trunks and root formations are natural and in good proportion, and an extremely handsome tree results. However there is one difficulty about seeds—one never knows whether the trees will be male or female. An important point if only one kind is wanted. In that case they are grafted.

In grafting, two or three year old seedlings are used for the base stock. If female trees are wanted a branch is selected that has fruited consistently over a period of years and cuttings made from this. They are generally about three inches in length. But as usual, try as hard as one may, the scars and bumps of the grafting show. In order to avoid this, layering is resorted to, making the top part of a branch into a new tree, but again, the roots are not well formed and other roots must be grafted on. So no matter what one does it takes years to make a good tree. As Ginkos have straight trunks the dwarfed kinds follow this shape. Generally they are planted singly but can be combined in groups. The pots used conform to the mass of the tree. Single specimens might have slightly deeper pots than groupings.

Repotting is done from the latter part of February to the middle of March. Once every two or three years is sufficient. Potting soil is four parts good earth, leaf mold two parts, sandy clay four parts, all well mixed. After repotting, place in a sunny location and after a couple of weeks give dilute liquid fertilizer. Don't neglect waterings.

The Ginko likes a sunny location with good circulation of air and protection from the burning western sun.

When the Spring growth becomes too long trim back to two or three buds. In trimming try to cut off the large leaves and from the cut bases two new leaves of smaller size will grow. This trimming strengthens the new buds and the branches will become stronger.

As Autumn approaches, be sure the trees have constant care and when cold weather comes expose them to one or two good frosts, when the leaves will of their own accord turn a magnificent golden color. They are then placed in a protected location out of the wind and enjoyed for their beauty. After the leaves have fallen they are moved to the Winter storehouse and kept out of the cold as they are especially subject to freezing.

## 10.  ILEX SERRULATA

### (Umemodoki) *Falling Scarlet Frost*

This variety of Ilex is generally seen in the old temple gardens of Japan, growing among rocks and at the bases of trees. It is an extremely ornamental shrub with an elegant and antique appearance. From Autumn and through Winter it is greatly enjoyed especially on snowy mornings, with the soft fluffy

A

B

*Ilex serrulata*

A.  *Berries clustered on the newer growth of an old, severely pruned tree.*

B.  *A younger, but excellently formed specimen.*

snow lightly powdering the scarlet berries. There are two kinds, those with scarlet berries and those with white. The scarlet kind is most generally cultivated. The berries are the chief attraction but the angular form of the shrub with its ancient bark is very good indeed. Propagation is generally from the berries.

The shape to which it is dwarfed are the Straight Trunk, Multiple Trunks, Cliff Style and Informal Groupings. The Straight Trunk and Informal Grouping effects are planted in shallow pots, while the Cliff Style takes a deeper container.

Each year they are repotted in early Spring while still dormant. Potting soil is sandy clay three parts, leaf mold one part, and river sand one part, all well mixed. Care is taken to assure good drainage.

If the new branches are not allowed to grow vigorously they will not set berries. The practice is to let the branches grow naturally until about June when the new berries can be seen and then the branches are trimmed back to the desired shapes. After this first general pruning other corrections can be made as new growth develops.

Wiring is extremely difficult. Do not try to wire the new sprouts as they break easily. Also the *Ilex serrulata* likes considerable water and this point cannot be neglected or the flowers or berries will fall.

After the flowers are finished dilute liquid fertilizer is given once or twice. As this shrub does not mind the cold it is left outside in the frost, when the berries turn a beautiful scarlet.


# 11.  JAPANESE ELM

## (Keyaki) *Zelkova serrata*

The Japanese Elm is becomming quite popular in the West. To those familiar with the huge Elms of New England the idea of having one of these mammoth trees reduced to miniature size is surely appealing. The Japanese Elm is mostly grown for the enjoyment of its bare shape in Winter, but its yellow leaves are also beautiful in Autumn. Among those Elms are large-leaved, medium-leaved and small-leaved kinds. There are also the green sprouting and the red sprouting. Those used for dwarfing are invariably the small-leaved, red sprouting kind.

The best Japanese Elms are raised from seed, although this takes a good many years. Those made by layering have poorly shaped roots and are not of much value. In raising from seed, the seeds are always taken from old mature trees which make a high percentage of narrow-leaved and red sprouting seedlings. Seeds are sown in Spring about the time of the Spring equinox. An ordinary flat filled with a mixture of earth and sandy clay is used. Seeds are planted closely and are barely covered. After sprouting they are moved into small pots and left for a year. Then they are repotted the second time and their main tap roots cut off, encouraging growth of surface roots.

The Japanese Elms are leaf trimmed several times a year, always working toward the general pattern of a mature tree.

Repotting is in early Spring. Remove excess roots, cutting back the earth from around the edges of the pots. Repotting earth is loamy soil five parts, sandy clay three parts and sand two parts. After repotting give considerable water. The application of dilute liquid fertilizer from time to time is beneficial.

As leaves on upper branches are strong and those on lower branches weak, one must constantly thin out excess leaves to balance growth. It is best not to use wires on the Elm, but if they must be put on, do so very loosely so as not to cut the bark.

If there are trees with roots on one side only, other roots can be started by cutting the cambium layer on the vacant side and tying the wound with moss, kept wet. In many cases roots will grow into the moss. This takes about six months. After the leaves have fallen the trees are admired for their shapes. Roots are injured by freezing so Elms are kept in winter storage.

*Japanese Elms are great favorites. This bonsai was made from the stump of a fairly large tree.*

## 12.  JASMINE

### (Robai) *Jasminum odoratissima*—Wax Plum

One of the romantic shrubs seen throughout our Southland and often mentioned in popular melodies is the Jasmine. Considered more of a vine than a tree, Western nurserymen would never believe it could be trained into a dwarfed form but the Japanese have long done this very thing. Their popular name for it is the "Wax Plum" because of the shape and texture of the yellow blossoms. It blooms at the same time as the Plum trees, and has a perfume stronger than that of any other Spring flower. In a season of damp and cold its golden color and fragrance are especially welcome. It was originally a native of China. The blossoms are rather large, the color is a real deep yellow and when placed in a large room it continues to bloom and scent the atmosphere for almost a month. The Jasmine has always been greatly esteemed.

As the Jasmine blooms heavily year after year, it must be repotted every Spring. The beginning to the middle of April is best in colder climates. The plant is removed from the pot, the roots trimmed carefully with at least fifty percent of the old earth left undisturbed. Potting soil consists of coarse garden earth four parts, sifted sandy clay four parts and leaf mold two parts. Be sure to place a layer of coarse gravel (about a fourth of the pot) in the bot-

*Jasmine is not usually thought of as a tree but here time and patience have done the unexpected.*

tom of the container for good drainage, as this is especially important with Jasmine.

Place in a sunny location where the Spring sunshine will bring out the abundant blooms. Give plenty of water. Later in the season when the blooming period is finished, place in the usual location with morning sun and afternoon shade. Through the Summer months it should be given a light fertilizing every two or three weeks. The Jasmine likes considerable fertilizer.

In Spring the Jasmine sends out many new shoots. Up to about April the new growth can be trimmed back to a couple of joints but after this time only cut off the really long shoots as next year's blooms form on the late growth.

Even though the Jasmine blooms in Winter, it dislikes cold so it is cultivated outside until about November and then moved into a sunny location well protected from Winter winds. It is vitally important that Winter watering be faithfully done. When in full bloom move the Jasmine into a warm but somewhat shady location and every two or three days take it out into the morning sun for a couple of hours.

## 13.  JASMINE

### (Obai) *Jasminum nudiflorum*—Golden Plum

The *Jasminum nudiflorum* is another variety that makes beautiful dwarfed trees. The Japanese have an appropriate name for it—"Geishunka" "The Flower That Goes to Welcome Spring" as it blooms so early in the season. In order to accomplish this it sets buds in October. The charming flowers are yellow and trumpet shaped, blooming in considerable profusion.

This variety is repotted every year in the Fall, the latter part of September being best. Potting soil is composed of seven parts of leaf mold and three parts of river sand, well mixed. After repotting, put the plant in a protected place for about twelve days then gradually bring it out into its usual location. As the weather becomes colder move it into a warm place well protected from frost.

In Spring new sprouts grow very rapidly but leave the plant alone until the height of Summer, then trim it back to shape. From then on do not do any more trimming as it will destroy next year's blooming wood. When the tree becomes older it develops branches that easily die back. So from about April when the plant seems to grow an inch or so a day, cut back the new growth leaving only one or two joints. If this type of trimming is done until about May it will help but one must not cut from then on.

Wiring is done in early Spring before the sprouts begin to grow. As the bark is very tender, be careful. Loosen the wires in Autumn.

Always watch the earth to see that it does not dry out and fertilize with dilute liquid manure. It is well to stop fertilizing during the season of greatest growth but to resume after Spring is past, fertilizing every month or so until September. As the plant grows quickly it needs considerable fertilization.

## 14.  MAPLES

(Yamamomiji) *Acer palmatum*—Mountain Maple
(Uchiwa Kaede) *Acer japonicum*—Fan Maple
(Hana Kaede) *Acer rubrum*—Flower Maple
(Tokaede) *Acer trifidum*—Trident Maple

In the Northern hemisphere the Maple is without question the most beloved tree of Autumn. America has no other foliage display approaching the glory of the flaming masses of color presented by groves and single specimens of Maple trees. There is no time of the year when Maples are uninteresting or unsightly. The new foliage of Spring resembles flowers; the green foliage of Summer is cool and refreshing; Autumn sees the trees in their unrivalled blaze of fiery beauty and Winter discloses their cleanly formed trunk and limb patterns. Truly the Maples are a satisfactory group and since antiquity have held their place in the literatures of both East and West.

Needless to say the Japanese likewise love Maples. They have developed varieties too numerous to count and ranging in size from the largest to the smallest. The leafing habits of these vary from almost solid forms to some resembling threads more than leaves. The varieties of Maples suited to dwarfing are many but in general the *Acer palmatum* variations are used.

The culture of the dwarfed Maples is rather troublesome. As they form such a mat of roots and quickly exhaust the soil, they are generally repotted every year while dormant. The potting earth is good garden soil to which enough sand has been added to assure drainage. There are some who maintain that if one wants to preserve the true elegance of the trees, they should not be repotted so frequently and this can be managed by judicious fertilization, lengthening the repotting interval by five or six years.

Trimming is a continual necessity in Maples. They have the habit of growing all season long and rapidly lose their shape. Start pinching new leaves in late Spring but not before, as there is considerable bleeding, so it is better

*Japanese Maples—Trident Maple in a
stylish container.*

*Above—Maple reaching far over its shallow pot.*

*Below—The Maples display their forms to great advantage in Winter.*

to shape the tree before the leaves appear.

In order to assure colorful Autumn foliage, place the trees in sunshine until about the first of June; then as the Summer sun becomes too strong, reduce the hours of sunshine or protect the trees with lath. Take special care to see they are not exposed to the late afternoon glare as the sun at this time is strongest, and will shrivel the ends of the Maple leaves, spoiling their beauty for the entire year.

In forming the shapes of Maples the trees should be designed to have the carefully regulated quality of a painting. In their bare state they should resemble scale drawings of natural trees.

Soft wire is used to train the trees and is applied in Spring. It is well to first wind the wire with paper. If too stiff wire is used or if the bare wire is not protected, injury may be done the tender bark. These wounds do not heal properly so it is well to take precautions.

The most popular shapes used in the training of Maples are Straight Trunk, Hanging Cliff, Roots Clasping Stones, and Multiple Trunk. In fact they look well in almost any style. Of late the most popular are those in which varieties with small leaves are planted in groves, or trained over rocks, either singly or in groupings. As the planting on rocks is especially suited to the character of Maples, various dwarfed tree lovers have vied with one another in creating beautiful effects in this manner. The very small 'bean size' dwarfed Maples are exceedingly popular. By using varieties with tiny leaves and training them to interesting shapes, they make most successful miniatures.

Here it would be well to mention the Trident Maple (*Acer trifidum*) as it is one frequently dwarfed. It has the habit of forming spectacular roots on the surface of the soil, so it is wonderfully adapted to Raft Style in shallow containers. Its foliage is trident shaped, hence the name, and if the first crop of leaves is picked off in June or July when the new growth has somewhat hardened, a second, smaller set will soon grow, giving the tree a good coloring in Autumn.

The Trident Maple grows quickly and vigorously, so must be constantly pinched back, and frequently repotted. The latter work is done each Spring, at which time most of the roots formed the previous year are cut off.

## 15.  JAPANESE MAPLES
### (Yama Momiji) *Acer palmatum*

The Yama Momiji are the small leaved kinds known as 'Japanese Maples' in the West. They are rather shrub-like in form, seldom growing over fifteen feet tall, while the foliage is beautifully notched and colored. They are attractive the entire year and especially so in Spring and Autumn, both seasons being referred to in Japanese as 'flowering.'

They are mostly propagated by seeds. Although seeds may be planted in flats, there are usually dozens of young trees to be found under the mature

ones.   These little seedlings have all the variations in foliage and coloring possible.   If dug in their dormant season after the leaves have fallen they may
be immediately potted and started on their way to becoming dwarfed trees.
The leaves are of good substance and can stand a fair amount of sunshine but
must be protected from the hot Summer sun.

The Yama Momiji needs considerable thinning and pinching back to preserve its shape and create a silhouette for the Autumn coloring.   At times old
branches can be removed to the general benefit of the tree's form.   When
shortening branches be sure to leave a pair or two of leaves on the new growth.
If all the new growth is trimmed off the tree does not do well.

Some types of the Yama Momiji have larger leaves than most.   In that
case when the new growth starts, pick off the largest leaves and as the season
progresses the newer foliage will be smaller.   Even if the new leaves are not
greatly reduced in size thinning will make them seem more in scale with the
rest of the tree.

Repotting is done annually about the time of the Spring equinox or earlier,
before the new growth has started.   The potting soil is composed of five parts
garden soil, sandy clay three parts, and two parts sand, well mixed.   The Yama
Momiji needs excellent drainage as its roots grow at such a rate that if sand
is not added to the potting mixture, the pot soon becomes a solid mass of roots
and drainage suffers accordingly.   Also, the upper roots seem to grow faster
than the bottom ones, which causes nourishment to be cut off to portions of
the tree, and branches die.   If there is a tight group planting, insufficient
drainage will bring about root rotting and dead trunks.   After repotting see
that the Yama Momiji has sufficient moisture to encourage the formation of
new hair roots.

The Yama Momiji requires a little more fertilizing than the other Maples.
Liquid fertilizer is applied once or twice in early Spring, after the foliage has
sprouted.   When the weather becomes warm, fertilization is stopped, but resumed in Autumn.   If this is faithfully attended to the Yama Momiji will have
wonderfully fine coloring in late Autumn.

As this kind of Maple sends out bursts of foliage two or three times a
season, there are ample opportunities to trim to a good shape.   If they are
not drastically thinned and pinched back the branches become entwined and
too dense.   Be sure to thin the small branches.

Wiring is done after the new growth has hardened a bit.   The bark is soft,
so the wires should be put on as loosely as possible.   The Yama Momiji must
be protected from late afternoon glare or the heat of Summer, but will stand
morning sun if kept watered.

Pests are few.   Aphids sometimes attack the young sprouts.   A good idea
is to keep most of the new growth cut off, and water the trees every evening,
spraying the under sides of leaves.   This will do away with the aphids in two
or three days.

## 16.  PEACHES
### (Momo) *Prunus persica*

In recent years most new Western gardens have included one or two Flowering Peaches in their planting.  There are now quite a number of varieties on the market, ranging in color from pure white to deep crimson.  Most are double, and are an important addition to our Spring color.  Strangely enough, with the exception of the little Peach trees sold on the streets in Japan in Spring and already mentioned, the Japanese do not often include these in their dwarfed tree collections.  Perhaps it is that the gorgeousness of the blossoms does not fit in with the Japanese ideas of elegance.  Nevertheless Westerners could find in the Peach a colorful addition to their Spring flowering dwarfed trees.

Peaches are propagated by planting seedlings and grafting established varieties onto these.  In addition to grafting, budding works well but does not supply a ready-made branch.

As the trees are grafted, their shapes are seldom good, so the beauty of the Peach would lie in its blossoms.  Trimming consists of removing sprouts from the main root stock and regulating the length of flowering wood.

Repotting is done every year in Spring or Autumn.  Early Spring is best. In repotting discard half of the old earth and cut off the surplus roots. Coarse sandy earth is placed in the bottom of the pot over a layer of gravel and trees are planted in a mixture of six parts black loam, sand two parts and leaf mold two parts.  It is important to give plenty of water.

After repotting place the Peaches in a sunny location with a good circulation of air.  Be especially careful in giving plenty of water.  If neglected at this time the trees will not do well.  On the other hand watch the drainage carefully.  If the earth in the pot becomes soggy for any length of time the trees will not bloom.  Fertilize after the trees have finished flowering and again in September and October to prevent branches dying in Winter.

A further note on pruning:  Be sure to leave two or three buds each time a branch is shortened.  If pruning is faithfully carried out it will aid in branching and the production of more flower growth.

Wiring is done in Spring but one must be careful and not knock off any buds.

Peaches cannot stand much cold and should be protected in the Winter. Also various insects such as aphids, etc., are partial to Peach trees.

## 17.  PERSIMMON
### (Kaki) *Diospyros kaki*

To one who has travelled in the smaller villages of Japan no Autumn scene is complete without the heavily laden Persimmon trees displaying their beautiful leaves and fruit against the background of weathered thatched roofs.

They complement each other perfectly. The Camellia is considered the rustic flower of Spring and the Persimmon fills a similar place in Autumn.

There are a great number of varieties but the tree found in most villages, called the Mountain Persimmon is the one most frequently used for dwarfing. In its native state the fruit is astringent but is set on the branches in an agreeable way and hangs on most of the year. There is a miniature version of the Mountain Persimmon called the Mame Gaki (Bean Persimmon) with fruit that occurs in small clusters but this has the defect of taking a long time to make a thick trunk.

Propagation is by seed or grafting. The usual method is by seed, unless special varieties are desired.

There are two times for repotting. In the Spring before the new growth appears and again in Autumn as soon as the leaves have dropped. Potting is done as seldom as possible. Every two or three years should be sufficient.

Potting soil is seven parts leaf mold and three parts coarse sandy clay. Be sure to put coarse gravel in the bottom of the pot. Trim the ends of the roots carefully. With warmer weather the new sprouts grow rapidly and when the new twigs are an inch or so in length put on wires, extending them as the twigs lengthen. If this is done the twigs will thicken and produce flowers. When the flowers begin to open, watering of the roots must be diligently attended to as this is the time the fruit sets. If it rains put the tree under shelter so the pollen will not be washed away. These are necessary precautions.

New sprouts grow rapidly. Unwanted ones are removed at the trunk or two or three joints out from the trunk. The remaining new branches are trimmed up after the fruit sets.

In the making of tiny dwarfed trees from small fruiting kinds one leaves a considerable number of fruits but when making a dwarfed tree of the large fruiting kind the tree is weakened if too many are left and affected in its setting of fruit for the following year. At first thin to about eight and when the fruit has definitely set make a final thinning to five. Don't allow the fruit to form on the same branches each year. Try to let branches rest a couple of years between fruitings.

Watering must be done evenly, guarding against drying. Persimmons are fertilized in Spring. Dilute commercial or animal manures are used. From late Spring to August fertilizing can be omitted but in September give a heavier application for the sake of the fruits, and stop fertilizing after the display season is over.

Give the tree plenty of sunshine. If it becomes weakened let it go for a year or so without bearing fruit, remove it from its pot and plant it in a sunny location in the field. When recovered it can again be repotted.

Scale is the chief pest. If possible don't spray with insecticides but try to eliminate by brushing and washing with water. Spray sometimes causes the fruit to drop.

*Flowering Plums (Apricots).*

A. *Postcard showing aged Plum from the Hikone Collection. (Flowers deep pink, lighter centers.)*

B. *Another unbelievable specimen from the same collection. (Blossoms are white.)*

C. *Weeping Plum in a tall pot.*

## 18.  PLUMS

*(Ume)  Prunus mume* Flowering Apricots—Flowering Plums

In California where Spring brings white clouds of Plum blossoms to countless orchards, the thought of dwarfing a single Plum tree is rather far-fetched.  Americans, and especially Californians have a habit of doing things on a large scale, but in Japan the cultivation of individual miniature Plums solely for their aesthetic appeal is a popular pastime.  Anyone with an appreciation of pure beauty soon finds that dwarfed Plum trees offer much of interest.

The shape of the trunks and branches are neat and attractive.  The trees bloom in snow and chilling winds, and hold their own against the elements.  Many have delicate fragrance.  In comparison with trees which do not materially change throughout the years, the Plum is truly attractive.

Ancient Japanese literature is filled with references to dwarfed Plums; some kinds we can still identify, but many have vanished through the centuries.  Undoubtedly most of these were originally derived from the wild *Prunus mume* or Field Plum (Yabai) and were for the most part white but after years of cultivation a considerable range of coloration was recorded.  One reads of deep reds, pale reds, lavender, pale yellow, greenish, striped red and white and so on.  Of course the white and deep red and many others are still familiar, but such kinds as the Lavender Plum, which was red striped with lavender, the Pale Yellow Plum, the Plum with the deep yellow of the *Kerria japonica,* the deep Lavender Colored Black Plum, and many other varieties have either completely vanished, or are so rare as to be objects of great rejoicing if discovered.

In feudal times the lords of the different provinces had wonderfully fine collections of dwarfed Plum trees.  Practically all of these have now died out or have been dispersed, but until recently there was still one remarkably complete collection remaining at a village near the Kaga Shrine out of Hikone.  Years ago I had the great fortune of seeing these ancient trees at their best.  There about two hundred specimens on display in a special building, and perhaps as many more had been taken from their pots for a rest and planted in the adjoining gardens.  They were amazing.  Some had relatively small trunks but others gnarled and at least a foot in diameter stood eight feet high in their containers.  All were labeled with fanciful names, such as Dragon Gate, Shining Jewel, Sunrise on the Sea, Flower of the Snowy Moon, Cascading Stars, and so on, but strange to say, the plants were so beautiful that the names didn't seem in the least exaggerated.  It was a constant marvel to see the aged and half decayed trunks, apparently with no roots to speak of, sending out vigorous new branches, completely covered with the most exquisite blooms of all descriptions and degrees of fragrance.  As at all such places, packs of postcards illustrating individual trees were sold, and as I write I have an assortment before me. On one of them I had drawn lines in pencil, indicating how the sprays of blossoms had grown even since the photograph had been taken. The pictures accompanying this chapter illustrate a couple of these trees. As this collection was almost the only one of its kind left in Japan, it was certainly well worth visiting. It included all colors and shapes; some of the more beautiful being the showering types, with streaming branches reaching from near the ceiling to the very floor. The owners had a large chart of the trees on display, with their names and classifications all set down, for the student of Japanese to decipher at his leisure. Sad to say this fine collection was accidentally burned in the destruction of an American Officer's Club, where the trees had been used for decoration.

Modern growers of dwarfed Plums roughly divide them into three classifications: white, red and variegated. There are so many kinds of Plums falling under these headings that an accurate estimate of their numbers is impossible. Perhaps sixty or more are in general cultivation, though some say as many as 500 could be found not so many years ago. In recent times the kinds used for dwarfing have greatly decreased in number. Following are some of the more common ones, with brief descriptions. While the exact varieties are hard to determine, the descriptions are fascinating and give an excellent picture of the qualities desired by Japanese dwarfed tree enthusiasts.

### YABAI (Field Plum) *Prunus mume*

The most universally distributed of the plums, sometimes incorrectly called 'Noume,' and the kind most frequently mentioned in ancient literature. Flowers are single, with five white petals. The best variety for dwarfing.

### KAGA HAKU (Kaga White Plum)

Another variety of the Yabai. Its special point is the beauty of its bark. A conventionalized design of this blossom was adopted as the family crest of the Lords of Kaga, where many of these trees were to be found, hence the name. Needless to say, it is a superior variety.

### KUNBAI (Fragrant Snow)

Still another variation of the Yabai. The flowers are so white that one would amost take them to be snow. Another good point is their exceedingly strong perfume. The single-petaled flowers make interesting circles.

### ZANGETSU BAI (Plum-of-the-Waning-Moon-in-the-Morning-Sky)

In the bud stage the unfolded petals are suffused with a beautiful reddish tinge; when open they turn pure snow white. Flowers are single, but larger than usual, opening around the New Year or a little later. The name 'Plum of the Waning Moon in the Morning Sky' comes from the color of the buds becoming paler as the flowers unfold, just as the moon's light fades in the early morning sky.

## KAN BAI (Cold Weather Plum)

The so-called early blooming variety. Another name is the Great Snow Plum (Dai Setsu Bai). It is single and white and a little larger than the Yabai. Like several other kinds it does not wait until Spring to open.

## SHO BAI (Little Plum)

From the Province of Koshu. The true variety has fruits that are narrow and long and though they are small, there is still considerable meat on them. As it is a smaller edition of the Yabai it is generally called the Little Plum.

## REBAI (Bell Plum)

Resemble the Yabai. Flowers are single, large and white. Six-petaled kinds are occasionally seen. Its fruit at the time of ripening hangs like the little round bells called 'Suzu' (round bells with a slit across the bottom seen on Santa Claus suits). When fully ripe the meat of the plums splits away from the kernels, adding the final touch of resemblance to the suzu. They bloom from New Years.

## KINBAI (Golden Plum)

Sometimes called the Green Willow Dyed Plum. It approaches yellow in color, some even resembling the *Kerria japonica*. The name Green Willow Dyed comes from the fact that the new foliage somewhat resembles that of a Willow.

The Plums generally used in the making of dwarfed trees are the Yabai (Field Plums). They are the best, developing beautiful colors, with the appearance of age on their trunks and limbs. The Hassaku Bai (First of August Plum) and the Toji Bai (Winter Solstice Plum) are also used in considerable numbers. The other, less widely known kinds are seldom seen, but interesting to know about. In general there are more white than red kinds and more single than double, as the enthusiasts have always liked the single varieties.

Spring is the longest season for the enjoyment of the Plum when the trees bloom over quite a period. In Summer they give pleasure with their fruits. Even Autumn and Winter have their attractions; some foliages turning delightful colors before falling. The gnarled trunks and branches show to greatest advantage in the cold weather.

If dwarfed Plums are placed in a greenhouse for forcing without first being exposed to one or two good frosts the results are not particularly good. It is the same as if native Plums in the field were denied their period of exposure to Winter's cold before being aroused to bloom by the warmth of Spring. If there is a cold room, it is best to first place them there from the outdoors, and then into a warm room. The kinds that burst suddenly into bloom and as rapidly finish, the Winter Solstice varieties, the cold weather blooming kinds, are best put directly out in the garden and then moved to the warm room. If the early blooming varieties are forced to flower even earlier the leaves are made to grow too quickly, springing out to a considerable length before the blossoms open.

The rules of cultivation say that those kinds that drop their leaves early in Autumn are easiest to handle and those that refuse to drop their leaves must be stripped about the month of October to encourage full flowering the next Spring. This refers exclusively to the early blooming kinds, especially the Hassaku Bai (First of August Plum) and similar varieties. If these kinds have their leaves stripped off early they bloom early the following season. Again if their period of transplanting is hurried a little and their leaves are stripped off in September they can even be forced to bloom in October. A good time for this early transplanting would be immediately following the normal period of bloom; that is about the middle of March when the blossoms have faded and the new leaves have not yet come out. If the leaves have formed and transplanting is attempted the tree is almost certain to die. April, May, June and July are months in which transplanting should not be done.

At the time of transplanting the early flowering kinds are considered individually with reference to the development of their buds. Those further along are attended to first. One must take care not to injure the roots unduly, cutting them as little as possible. Only remove the roots that are growing out at unwanted angles or are exposed and those winding around the inside edges of the pots. Some growers of dwarfed trees wait until the Plums have finished blooming, then take them from their pots without breaking their balls of earth and with a hatchet chop off excess roots on all four sides. Then they are repotted with fresh earth. In some cases this treatment is perfectly safe but it is well to remember that if too many roots are removed at repotting time, branches will start growing with great speed and the shape of the tree will suffer.

Loam, sandy clay and sand mixed are used in repotting. Proportions are: Loam (dust sifted out and discarded) seven parts; sandy clay (also dust sifted out) three parts. In this mix an amount of sand sufficient to make the soil porous so water will readily seep through. In the bottom of the pot place a quantity of gravel for drainage.

Plums require considerable fertilization to aid blooming. Solutions of commercial and animal fertilizers are used. The most satisfactory period for their application is from late Spring to early Summer. Dilute solutions given twice or three times a month should be sufficient.

After the middle of Summer the development of the leaf buds will serve to indicate where the flowers for the following season are apt to appear. Keeping this in mind, wind branches to be trained with the proper wires but avoid all buds. If the plants are being grown for flowers, late Summer is best but if the blossoms are of no importance the wires may be put on in Spring.

If the new leaf buds of Plums are pinched back there is danger of destroying the flower buds too. If the new growth is pinched back in May, there will be no flowers and if the pinching back is done too early there will be a second growth and the whole thing will have to be done over again. So it is advisable to wait until late Autumn and then give the trees a thorough pruning. After pruning place the trees in a location with a good circulation of air and exposure to full sunlight for a considerable portion of the day. As to watering, at the time of the heavy Spring rains, slacken the watering just after heavy downpours and allow for a little drying; but give plenty of water in Midsummer to keep the soil from burning and drying.

The insects that do greatest damage to Plum trees are the various scales. Several decades ago these were particularly feared as at that time no real method of combating them had been worked out and whole collections were destroyed. Now however effective sprays are on the market and there is not the great dread of this pest that formerly prevailed.

The tiny 'bean size' Plums are easily made: those little dwarfed trees that, pot and all can be held in one's hand. The Japanese have the expression "Eighteen years for the Plum to bloom." This applies to practically all kinds (with one or two exceptions) when raised from seed, but there is a short cut in the making of the tiny kinds.

If little dwarfed Plums are made from cuttings, they may be completed in about three years, and after five or six years present all the characteristics of good dwarfed trees.

Make the cuttings when the parent trees have about finished blooming, and the leaves are starting to bud. Select vigorous last year's wood, trim the cuttings into lengths of seven or eight inches, and with a sharp knife or shears make a clean cut across the lower end of each piece, then turn the cuttings over and make a slight cut from the opposite side eliminating all rough edges. Split or otherwise damaged cuttings from Plums do not root. As too short cuttings from Plums do not root, be sure to make them around seven to nine inches long. It is best to prepare them a year in advance.

To do this select twigs on the mother tree with good curves or shapes, shapes that will eventually become the patterns for the new tree. However, as curved and shapely twigs are rare, one usually selects straight pieces and trims them as desired, so they will have somewhat formed the required shapes by the following Spring when they will be cut from the parent tree. As nine out of ten cuttings put in the pots die, the best method is to make a cold frame or bed directly in the ground and place the cuttings two-thirds deep in the soil. To make the bed select an out-of-the way spot where drainage is good and there is considerable sunshine. Dig the earth to a depth of eighteen inches, breaking it up well and mix the upper part with sand.

The more vigorous cuttings will probably root before the following Autumn and grow a foot or two into the bargain. At that time, or the following Spring (Spring is best) they can be trimmed back to the shapes previously decided upon and from then on trimmed as required. Give a sufficient amount of fertilizer and as the new wood forces itself out, keep it trimmed so the shape of the projected tree is gradually approached. The new dwarfed trees may be lifted and potted the following Spring.

To help the limbs and trunk to thicken feed the tree on rich leaf mold or well fertilized earth for about three years. If this is done the chances are the tree will bloom its third Spring. From then on one can change over to the usual care given dwarfed trees. In following out this method of making miniature trees from cuttings it is well to stick to the Yabai (Field Plum). Other kinds are at times impossible to root.

## 19.  POMEGRANATE

### (Zakuro) *Punica granatum*

The Pomegranate has long been used in the Near Eastern, Indian, Chinese and Far-Eastern landscaping and as a subject for painting and textile design. Persian miniatures generally include Pomegranates in their garden scenes and many Indian prints have motifs based on the Pomegranate. This is not surprising as it is such a beautiful tree. Not only are the flowers and fruits exceedingly ornamental but the leaves and especially the texture and shape of the trunk are most unusual. The Japanese are skilled in the making of dwarfed Pomegranates that reflect all the splendid qualities of the full sized tree.

The Pomegranate is both a fruiting and a flowering dwarfed tree. There are many varieties divided roughly into two categories. There is the 'Tenshin Omi' (Tenshin—large fruited) which has the largest fruit, up to three inches in diameter. Another variety called 'Suisho Omi' (Crystal fruited) is also divided into two kinds, the large-leaved and the small-leaved, but the best fruit is on the large-leaved which blooms in Summer with white flowers. The fruit is white and semi-transparent. Another kind, Hitoe Kaba (Single Brown) also has large or small leaves, but the fruit comes on the large-leafed kind.

Propagation is by hardwood cuttings taken in the Fall and rooted in the usual manner or by layering. Cuttings would be more convenient.

The pots used for Pomegranates could be somewhat more colorful than the average. As the Pomegranates bloom for a considerable portion of Summer, their bright orange flowers would harmonize well with pots glazed in paler greens and off-whites.

Trimming consists of thinning branches and removing surplus twigs to expose the main form of the tree. The Pomegranate makes dense heads of small twiggy growth. About half or two-thirds of this material should be trimmed out. Then the remaining leaves and flowers appear to greater advantage.

Pomegranates are repotted every two or three years or when root-bound. This is done in early Spring when the new red foliage is just beginning to

*Pomegranates*

    A.   *A tree in Summer, with its glisten-
        ing foliage.*

    B.   *The interesting textures of the bare
        Winter pattern.*

A

B

appear. Potting soil is six parts of sifted garden earth, three parts of sandy clay and one part river sand. After repotting give sufficient water and place in a protected spot for a couple of weeks. Pomegranates do not like too much water but the earth should never be allowed to really dry. When the Pomegranate is planted as a dwarfed tree, it sends out long branches. Unfortunately it flowers from the tips of these so the branches can not be cut off entirely. A satisfactory compromise is to remove the long branches that do not add to the shape of the tree and trim the others back two or three joints. When the tree is flowering, thin any fruits that might set to four or five so as not to overtax its strength.

The first of March is a good time for wiring. To protect the smooth bark insulated wire can be used. In Autumn after the fruit has dropped, one can give the tree a good going over.

After repotting, fertilize every month until the tree comes into bloom. Give liquid fish or chemical, well diluted. Fertilizing before the flowering season helps to set new fruit. After the flowering season starts do not fertilize. When the fruit has thoroughly set, until the first of October, fertilizing can be resumed. Protect from cold during Winter.

As for pests, aphids are about the only things to give much trouble and these can be controlled by washing off new growth with a stiff spray with the garden hose.

The Pomegranate is truly a spectacular tree and always attracts attention. To see a miniature tree with almost full sized fruit is an ever startling experience.

## 20. WEEPING WILLOW

### (Yanagi) *Salix babylonica*

The Weeping Willow is a familiar tree throughout the Western world. Noted for its remarkably rapid growth and beautifully pendant habit, it occupies a special place in gardening tradition and literature. Who has not heard of the "Willows of Babylon"?

Willows are especially beautiful in early Spring with their budding leaves and shoots and in Summer, clothed in cool green moving with the slightest breeze. While not spectacular, the yellow leaves of Autumn are colorful and the Wintry pattern of their naked branches against the sky is unique and can never be mistaken for that of any other tree. Altogether the Willow is delightful the entire year.

Fortunately these trees are among the easiest of all to root from cuttings. Just find a small or even fairly large branch with a good shape, saw it off and set it in a tub of water and sand. It invariably roots. Branches up to four inches in diameter have been started this way. Early Spring is the best time.

Watering is the most important point in the cultivation of the Willow. As it is a tree that likes wet earth one must at all times make sure that this condition is maintained. If watering is overlooked only once or twice, dead branches result, the tree loses its luster and the foliage takes on an unattractive appearance.

Repotting is somewhat later than for most dwarfed trees. April through May is best in colder climates, but the latter part of February would be better in California. Earth used is garden soil mixed with a considerable quantity of sand. However as the Willow sends forth great masses of roots there are times when the trees must again be repotted in Fall. After repotting give a good application of liquid fertilizer. If one puts on a little too much, it will do no harm.

Willows are an easy prey to aphids which gather on the undersides of branches and leaves. If aphids once become established, ants soon follow and, if left with no attention, the tree will lose it vigor. Aphids are easily controlled by spraying the under parts each evening with a fairly stiff force of water from the hose, and by pinching off the tips of the new foliage where most aphids congregate.

In Winter see that the trees continue to receive enough water. It is easy to neglect Willows at this season and if watering is neglected, branches will die.

The Japanese have a special way of planting Willows called "Root-Washing-Style." Trees are arranged in shallow containers of water among pebbles and earth. The white hair-like roots spread into the water and suggest coolness during the hot Summer season.

## 21. WISTERIA

### (Fuji) *Wisteria multijuga*—Japanese Wisteria

### *Wisteria chinensis*—Chinese Wisteria

When Spring comes to Western homes the chief glory of many gardens is the Wisteria arbor hung with masses of fragrant white or lavender racemes, their delicate and fragile beauty contrasting wonderfully with the old and gnarled trunks. The thought of dwarfing such monsters seems an impossibility but the Japanese have always loved the Wisteria as a dwarfed tree as well as in its natural condition.

The Wisteria is a native of Japan and China found growing in the hills and mountains. Upon being transplanted to gardens and trained, and one variety crossed with another, changes occurred and now there are many kinds. In addition to the original white and lavender, there are flowers of darker or lighter shades and a pinkish variety. Others have strong fragrance and racemes are of all lengths, up to as much as six feet. Following are some of the more popular kinds of Wisterias: (Japanese name: Fuji)

CHIEFUJI—This is the double variety, comes both in white and lavender, rare but not considered better than the single kinds.

JAKOFUJI—The flowers are milk white in color, have a good fragrance and when made into dwarfed trees and shown at exhibitions, have good design and perfume.  Sometimes called NIOIFUJI—'Fragrant Wisteria.'

KAPITAN FUJI—The clusters are pure white.  While the individual flowers are large, the racemes are short.  It is more suited for dwarfing than for planting in the garden.

KOFUJI (Little Wisteria) NATSUFUJI (Summer Wisteria)—The small leaves are more prized than the flowers.  In summer one places the plant in a water tray (suiban) or trains it over stones.  They are well suited for dwarfing.

KUCHIBENI (Rouge colored Wisteria)—The petals for this variety are tipped and veined with a bluish pink by degrees fading to white; near the stamens and pistils the flowers are completely cloudy white.

KUROFUJI (Black Wisteria)—Blossoms are of a deep violet color and as they have a black overcast, this accounts for the name.  The size of the individual flowers and length of the racemes is average.

NODAFUJI—Originated at Noda in Setsuhu Province.  Flowers are well arranged, the color is a pale lavender and the racemes are of excellent quality.

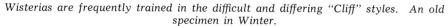

*Wisterias are frequently trained in the difficult and differing "Cliff" styles.  An old specimen in Winter.*

SHIRO NODAFUJI (White Noda Wisteria)—This came from the usual Wisteria, the color is milk white and the racemes sometimes reach a length of four or five feet.

TAIWANSAKKO (Formosan Wisteria)—Completely different from the usual Wisteria varieties. The flowers occur in short racemes and are of pinkish lavender color. The trunk takes on a fine antique appearance and as the plants bloom in Summer they are greatly prized.

YAMAFUJI (Mountain Wisteria)—There is the white and also a violet kind. The flowers have a beautiful antique style and are suited to dwarfing.

There are some interesting ideas about Wisterias. One old book says "If rice juice left over from making wine is poured on the roots, the plant will flourish." Some still believe that the pouring of Sake into the water of Wisteria flower arrangements will keep the flowers from wilting.

Propagation is carried out in several ways; by planting seed, by layering and by grafting. As raising the plants from seed takes a good many years, layering is chiefly used. However as many varieties are slow in forming roots, another method is to grow seedlings and graft established varieties onto these. Most Wisterias sold in nurseries have been grafted. While the bumps and scars remaining from this grafting are readily seen, they are not objectionable as the natural Wisteria trunks have much the same contours and, at the time of blooming, this even helps in the contrast of flowers and antique stems. If Wisterias are grafted on strong roots, the growth is speeded and in a few years well formed plants result.

Wisterias make huge fleshy roots, which form one of their principal charms and they also take about twice as much water as any other plant used in dwarfing. For these reasons they are kept in rather tall pots with sufficient space left for holding moisture. Shapes are mostly in the Cliff Style with Cascading effects. Occasionally a Wisteria will be planted in a shallow container because of its special beauty but in that case watering must be carefully attended to.

Trimming of the Wisteria is a continuing task. Whenever the long trailers appear, they should be cut back immediately to two or three buds as if one were trimming a Grape Vine. Wisterias trained into trees are forever trying to regain their vine shape.

There are two times when Wisterias can be repotted, Spring and Autumn. Both are good but if they are transplanted in the Spring it must be quite early. Earth used is good fertile soil in which some clay has been mixed. The Wisteria roots being thick and fleshy are easily cut and broken so sufficient care must be taken in this regard. Usually only the smaller roots are trimmed but if it is necessary to remove some of the large fleshy roots, cut them cleanly and squarely. If in repotting, large roots are torn, cut these afresh. After the plants have been repotted place them from five to ten days in a shady place. Do not fertilize sooner than two months after repotting.

Wiring is seldom needed. The branches are naturally gnarled and a slight pruning will generally be sufficient to maintain shape. If wiring should be a necessity, apply loosely so as not to cut into the soft bark.

When the plants begin to bud, take special care with the watering. Don't neglect but give plenty. It is even a good idea to place the pots in shallow trays of water about an inch deep. When the flowers have come out, trim back any new leaf shoots and keep the shape of the plant in good order. If the long trailers are allowed to grow, the form of the plant suffers and next year's buds will fail to set.

Fertilize with a dilute liquid manure or fish emulsion in late Summer. At the same time continue pruning or the plant becomes messy. As the Wisteria is usually trained in the style of a plant hanging from a precipice, the maintaining of this shape takes constant care.

Wisterias have remakably few pests. Chief difficulty is keeping them wet enough in hot weather. They sometimes have to be watered two or three times a day. If water is even once neglected the ends of the leaves curl inward, turn brown and are spoiled for the season.

The Formosan Wisteria is different from other kinds. It blooms in Summer. There are two varieties—pink and white. The racemes are well shaped. Its cultivation is the same as for the others. The flowers bloom from July to August and when they are finished, the seed pods are removed. While beautiful, they damage the plant. As the Formosa Wisteria was originally a tropical vine, it must have Winter protection. Like all other Wisterias you cannot give it too much water.

# BIBLIOGRAPHY

IN ENGLISH

Bonsai—Miniature Trees, by Claude Chidamian
        D. Van Nostrand Co., 1955.

The Art of Growing Miniature Trees, Plants, and Landscapes,
        by Tatsuo Ishimoto
        Crown Publishers Inc., NYC., 1956.

Handbook on Dwarfed Potted Trees,
        by Brooklyn Botanic Garden, 1953.

Bonsai—Japanese Tourist Library ♯ 13.
        Published by Japan Travel Bureau, 1950

The Japanese Art of Miniature Trees and Landscapes,
        by Yuji Yoshimura and Giovanna M. Halford.
        Published by Chas. E. Tuttle Co., Tokyo, 1957.

IN JAPANESE

Bonsai, by Kanai Shuin.  Published by Kosei-do Shoten, Tokyo, 1922.

Bonsai no Kenkyu, (The Study of Bonsai)
        by Kobayashi Kenyo.  Published by Haku-kun-ban, Tokyo, 1931.

Bonsai, by Miyasawa Bungo.  Published by Gen-shin-sha, Tokyo, 1923.

Bonsai no Shitate Kata, (How to Make Bonsai)
        by Bando Sumio.  Published by Kin-en-sha, Tokyo, 1954.

# INDEX

## — A —

## — B —

## — C —

## — D —

## — E —

## — F —

## — G —

## — R —

## — S —

## — T —

## — V —

## — W —

IMPORTED AND DISTRIBUTED BY
JAPAN PUBLICATIONS TRADING CO.
SAN FRANCISCO, CALIF., U.S.A.